Systemic Constellation Work
Is an Art
About Deep Dimensions of Family Therapy
A Collection of Essays by Heinz Stark
1999-2005

D1602300

The Stark Institute and Many Kites Press
© 2005 Heinz Stark

Published in cooperation with:
The Stark Institute
Duebbekold 10
D- 29473 Goehrde, Germany

Many Kites Press
3907 Minnekahta Drive
Rapid City, South Dakota 57702

Cover design by Antje Jaruschewski
Printed in the United States of America
With Booksurge Publishing
www.booksurgepublishing.com

ISBN 0-9729002-3-3

Acknowledgements

My first deeply felt gratitude goes to Bert Hellinger. The phenomenological Systemic Constellation Work that he initiated not only changed my therapeutic work fundamentally; it also literally saved my life. With the publication of my essays in the United States, I would like to use this occasion to thank all those whose dedication and organizational work provided the material foundation for the many valuable constellation experiences I have gathered in North America since 1995.

I would like to name some of these outstanding personalities: first we have Hunter Purdy, who made it possible for me to take my first steps in America as a facilitator of constellations in California, Kentucky, Florida, Arizona and Washington. I thank Tom Daly and Jude Blitz for paving the way for me in Colorado and Gary Riestenberg for doing the same in Minnesota. Diana Norman was successfully responsible for my access to South Dakota, and Jeanne Snyder, Sandy Zboyan and Dietrich Klinghart for the work in Seattle.

The wonderful two-year training in Southern California was organized and made possible by Margot Ridler, with whom I am connected in fruitful cooperation within the Orders of Life Association. John Gordon has my full recognition and gratitude for the generous grant that he donated to trainees in need. I would here also like to thank Ted Cowper, Helena Sprake, and Margarete and William Meiger for their organizational dedication and support dedication which made it possible for me to have many good experiences in workshops in California. I also want to thank Doug Garret in California who had organized the very first public workshop there after I led my first in house training at Esalen Institute.

On several occasions Wiep de Vries' house in Pasadena was a safe haven for me.

Milt and Jamie Lee handled the enormous organizational challenge surrounding the unforgettable experiences with constellation work with Lakota Indians in South Dakota; here, I would also like to especially thank the Pourier Tiyospaye (Clan) on the Pine Ridge Reservation.

I want to warmly thank Annette Aubrey in Alberta/Canada for bringing together the constellation groups in Canada. The workshops in Hawaii were made possible through the efforts of Nicolas Kern and his wife Anja.

Last, but not least, I send a bunch of thank-you flowers to the friends at the Healing, Heart and Soul Organization for the truly powerful training group in Wisconsin; here, I want to especially mention Sue Bronson, Betsy Collins, and Ron Anderson.

I want to thank Sophie Warning for doing the basic translation of the essay "The Return of the Shamans;" Sten Linnander did the main work translating all other texts. Suggestions for improvements were provided by trainees, especially by Annika Gruenn, Diana Yankelevitz, Gary Stuart, Ken Day and Chris Straw.

The book also profited greatly from the English skills of Betsy Collins in Milwaukee, Wisconsin and Andi Hummel in Hulett, Wyoming.

And finally, in this context I want to express my warm gratitude to the editors, especially Patricia Jamie from Many Kites Press in Rapid City, South Dakota. In Germany, Antje Moeller of the Stark Institute contributed to the success of the book project with secretarial work and e-mails, as did Antje Jaruschewski with her graphic work for the cover.

Table of Contents

Introduction. vii

1. The Return of the Shamans—About Dealing with Death and the Dead. 1

2. The Relationship of The Living and The Dead in Systemic Constellation Work. 25

3. The Art of Family Constellation: Conceptual Thoughts About High Quality Training. 43

4. Family Constellation On the Reservation. 67

5. The Embodied Family System. 89

6. Constellation Work with Cancer Patients. 101

7. Two Strategies—One Modality; Classical Constellation Work and Movements of the Soul, or "Movements of Spirit". 109

Introduction

Imagine having worked continuously as a therapist with a client and having achieved considerable success. The client now gets along well with her pubescent daughter, she takes care of herself consistently, and her inner separation from the dominant mother of her childhood has given way to self-confidence and straightforwardness. Episodes of hypochondria have largely abated and now, long after her divorce, she could again enter into a relationship with a man.

There was, however, one thing that resisted all therapeutic efforts and that was a longing for death that was almost lyrical and erotic. I applied body therapy according to Alexander Lowen's energetic observations regarding the longing for death; I delved into Freud's deep psychology hypothesis about the longing for death, I facilitated primal therapy regression work; I did spiritual healing aura work and used art therapy to allow the soul to express itself. All this provided some relief but could not truly help her overcome the symptoms.

When the daughter now also began to paint her room black, I decided to "pull the last ace out of my sleeve" and to stage her own funeral as psychodrama. It was eerie for all those involved, but not for our client; she enjoyed the event with great satisfaction.

I had finally used up my entire arsenal of methods that I had gathered until then. Some time later, during a session, I asked her to repeat after me two simple sentences. She did so, and it had an effect as if lightning had struck!

Her stress disappeared; her body, soul and spirit lightened up visibly, and tears of emotion flowed down her cheeks. We both felt the love that spread through the room.

The curse was broken and her symptom of longing for death went away forever on this day. Repeating two sentences solved a problem that ten years of full immersion into the healing waters of humanistic therapy could not touch. This was a turning point for her in her life and as a client, for it was the end of the therapy.

You can probably imagine that this resounding success jolted me and initiated a major shift in my therapeutic orientation. I was fascinated by the obvious beauty of the approach that combined great effectiveness with amazing simplicity. A new era had begun for me personally, too, and my own difficulties in life began to subside.

Parallel to my psychotherapy work, my art therapy and art courses and workshops, I took part in a new training group in Postural Integration (P.I.) according to Jack Painter, from 1989 to 1992. It was led by the trainers Irmtraud and Anton Eckert, who combined and expanded Jack's Postural Integration, consisting of Rolfing, Shiatsu and Gestalt Therapy (Fritz Perls), with essential elements of Reichian body psychotherapy (Wilhelm Reich, Alexander Lowen, Gerda Boyesen and others).

Driven by the desire to acquire healing tools that were as holistic as possible and by the nagging feeling that something essential was still missing inside of me, my existence, and my life, I kept traveling to the P.I. training sessions from Northern Germany, where I lived, to Southern Germany, where I was born. It was during this training that I suddenly ran into what at the time was still an entirely local South German phenomenon—a name that had created astonishment and excitement in the informed therapy scene: Bert Hellinger.

I heard one or the other amazing story, I experienced a rudimentary family constellation, and finally I heard an audio tape with a lecture that Bert had held close to Munich with the title: The Orders of Love. I copied the cassette and listened to it several times.

At first it affected me subconsciously, below the level of my attempts to learn Postural Integration. P.I. is a technically very demanding "hands on" method, and there was very much to learn. To me, Bert Hellinger's sentences sounded strange, as if they had been chiseled in stone and had been carried down from Mount Sinai by Moses to his unsuspecting people. In part, they were diametrically opposed to my leftist liberal way of thinking, and yet they affected me like a creeping infection, which ultimately afflicts all organs and finally also the brain and the soul— especially the soul.

This infection put me into an increasingly heated state of excitement and finally I decided to find out everything I could about it and to fulfill my longing for what was missing in my life. Today I am still learning. At the time, I was more in a state of astonishment and not as certain and as calm as I am today. But even now there is a sense of new beginnings and new discoveries in Systemic Constellation Work.

I hope that you sense some of this in the texts that I am presenting to you in this book, also something of my own awe, and of the enthusiasm that I of course at first wanted to share with the whole world. I remember that later, during my P.I. Master training in Southern France, I tried unsuccessfully to get Jack Painter to become enthusiastic about the "wonderful Systemic Constellation Work."

It was not until later that I became aware of what a great challenge this work represents, and how much of our liberal and very Anglo-Saxon/American therapy concepts we have to give up, if we truly want to get involved with the depths of phenomenological Constellation Work. It is not only our therapeutic concepts that are at stake, but our entire world view and our view of the human being, in which the isolated actions and efforts of the individual to attain happiness and self-realization constitutes the highest credo.

In the light of the discovery that our lives follow certain orders and that subconscious loyalties and balancing mechanisms affect us through the generations in a kind of common soul of our tribes and families, I found myself forced to give up a considerable number of methods and interventions that had been important to me in my therapeutic work. Other methods I had to at least reevaluate and subordinate to larger and further reaching insights.

In the case of our client with her longing for death, I was dismayed to realize that some of my measures must even have been counterproductive.

So what were the two wondrously effective sentences that I asked her to speak aloud?

They were: "My very dear father, you died in the war when I was still very small, I never got to know you, but my soul knows you and I am very much drawn to you, an intense longing draws me to you. I now take you into my heart and let you be very close to me here in life, and thus I will live with you in my heart for as long as I am permitted, and then I will come, too."

Simple, isn't it? Do you feel what kind of love this is all about?

Love is the essence of Constellation Work; all serious problems come from unconscious love and are solved with conscious love.

Most suicides that I have dealt with in Constellation Work follow exactly this pattern of following someone in death, either in order to be close to the beloved person that one maybe has not even heard of, and that therefore can be totally unknown at the conscious level, or else to save them from death by sacrificing one's own life.

Yes, that's right, the latter strangely archaic-sounding movement of the soul toward the dead not only relates to the living, in whose stead one is willing to die (even if the ego resists it), but in a strange elimination of linear time, it actually relates to the dead. I found many things in my life that were caused by such dynamics. In my own first constellation with Bert Hellinger I held my stillborn twin in my arms, and for the first time in my life I felt truly fulfilled. It was the beginning of a reunion with a whole row of ancestors and siblings, and with every new one I felt more complete.

Sacrificing one's own life for the sake of love, in favor of a person who is about to die, is familiar to us Christians through the behavior that is ascribed to Jesus. This religious desideratum would not be understandable to us normal mortals unless we ourselves potentially have these impulses in our soul.

If you wish to read and think more about such topics, which are not only therapeutically important, but also represent experiences of phenomenological Systemic Constellation Work that are significant in terms of cultural philosophy, then I invite you to read the essay "The Return of the Shamans."

It deals with nothing less than aspects of the archaic roots of our existence as human beings that still today operate in our souls, either extremely virulently or extremely beneficially. It presents experiences of Constellation Work regarding how we deal especially with the dead and with our ancestors, and how we can let them have a positive effect on us.

The wonderful thing about this phenomenological Constellation Work, where we fully entrust ourselves to the phenomenon, to that which appears, is that such facts, which go far beyond our everyday experiences, scientific research or theoretical concepts, can be experienced so simply.

We learn essential things about invisible connections, interrelationships and existential orientations through the induction into a social system (family) as representatives of relevant elements (persons).

This becomes especially exciting when dealing with those who have been dead for a long time. We suddenly find ourselves in noticeable resonance with their unredeemed actions and behavior during their lifetimes and with their violations of the orders of the soul that still today have an effect on us who are alive. As the connections and backgrounds that usually were unknown up until then become visible, it becomes possible to deal with problems posthumously in a sense.

In the text "The Relationship between the Living and the Dead in Systemic Constellation Work," you can find essential material about such surprising things and about how we who work with systemic constellations deal with them. In a sense, this text is a continuation and expansion of the previous essay "The Return of the Shamans."

With the publication of this text in our distinguished journal (Practice of Systemic Constellations), I have, hopefully in a balancing way, intervened in a heated discussion among those in the constellation scene. The discussion began when suddenly some persons, after years of dealing with death and the dead in constellations, were shocked to realize that we are constantly interacting with the dead. This was something that had been totally suppressed from our culture.

In this connection, it was necessary to examine all approaches and attempts at explaining how the transgenerational information phenomena occur. The essay is thus also a contribution toward a theory of phenomenological constellations.

If you have not yet experienced Constellation Work, it may be difficult for you to understand fully everything that is being discussed here. All the texts I am presenting to you here were addressed to a lively German and European constellation scene, with the intent of taking a stand regarding questions that have arisen as a result of spreading and deepening the work.

However, I believe and hope that you will have the same experience as I did when I heard Bert Hellinger's lecture on an audiotape. I hope that you notice the differences between the "common sense" way of understanding life and how we are taught by constellations to see life and human beings. This is a way of seeing that is totally new, and yet it touches on something very old, it is a way of seeing that is related to the soul and familiar to the heart.

Maybe you will feel the same way as the Lakota (Sioux) woman, who at the end of the workshop said: "We always knew what you are practicing here with us, we just forgot it."

The text about constellation experiences on the Pine Ridge Reservation (Family Constellations on the Reservation) may be a good introduction to the texts for American readers. In this text I deal with a burning problem in American reality, but I also describe experiences that make it possible for us to recognize far-reaching solutions. To me, this text seems best suited for newcomers to the wondrous world of intergenerational Constellation Work, since it tends to follow the American tradition of using a narrative style, even when dealing with factual issues, rather than the German manner of writing in a philosophical, analytical way.

However, what my American trainees have learned while going through the translations in the German style is, in addition to the content, it is necessary to pause for a moment and make an effort in order to descend into the depth of Hellinger-orientated living philosophy. Once you have become interested in Systemic Constellation Work, it should not be difficult for you to do what the trainees were able to do.

If you wish to understand the special requirements involved in a high quality training in Systemic Constellation Work, read my insights in the essay: "Family Constellation is an Art." In this text, my experiences as an adult educator and art teacher are merged with the training in Systemic Constellation Work. This text is also a rich source for practicing SCW facilitators to reflect on their own virtues and behavior in the constellation process.

As you may have noticed, I find it especially important to train one's own body as an instrument of perception. For this reason we deal with materialized, embodied character structures that I have begun to expand into systemic contexts. The present essay is a first contribution to this, and others are sure to follow. There are many body-oriented psychotherapists in Germany who, like me, have hit upon Constellation Work and are trying to combine it with their own traditional disciplines. I do this myself in my practice, with respect for both approaches. However, in recognition of the greater scope of phenomenological Constellation Work, I proceed in the opposite order: I follow the question of how insights from body therapy can be incorporated into the phenomenological systemic work. In this way, I slowly delve deeper into the emergence of a Systemic Integrative Therapy (SYIN).

Anyone who deals with the body naturally encounters bodily symptoms and thus the phenomenon of illness, or, broadly speaking, how our body speaks about malfunctions in the common soul body of our family system. In terms of frequency, symptoms of illness naturally represent an important part of our client's need for solutions. Almost everybody is affected in some way, be it only through the fear of a severe illness, such as cancer.

Recently I was asked to write a contribution for a book about alternative methods of healing cancer by the editors of a well-known talk show on German national TV that deals with problems in life and where I have often represented the position of systemic family constellations in regards to various life problems. I did not want to deny you this contribution, since it again shows in a striking way how we are entwined in love with the fate of those that belong to us in the realm of the living and the dead.

Although the essay "Two Strategies, One Modality" is the next to the last in terms of the sequence of publication, I would like to present this work at the end of this collection, since it is a treatise that points to a possible common future of the constellation movement. In it, I deal with important divergences in the mode of operation and in the philosophical evaluation of the Systemic Constellation Work, which are more suited to split and fragment the movement and that do not let many kites fly in the same wind, which used to be our pride. In this essay I also provide insights that may be important to many constellation facilitators and that are based on experiences of my own, such as the integration of the methods of movement ("movements of the Soul/movement of Spirit") and the classical constellation method.

May the wealth of my experience that I have laid out here benefit your work, your family and your life.

1
The Return of the Shamans—about Dealing With Death and the Dead[1]

I am firmly convinced that the restlessness that drives modern man has its roots in a disturbed relationship to the ancestors . . . Only chaos can arise from an unbalanced relationship between the living and the dead. —Malidoma Patrice Somé, African shaman[2]

During a seminar in 1995 at the Esalen Institute in California, the Australian dream expert Robert Moss, who had learned of my Family Constellation Work the evening before, told me that he had heard about the fantastic shamanic work that I had done. When I asked him, somewhat amazed, why he thought that my work was shamanic, he told me that he had heard that I had worked with the dead.

During a course in Seattle in 1997, a female participant asked me what the difference was between Hellinger work and shamanism. I answered that we had a different way of working with the dead and we did not have to leave this realm and enter into the realm of the dead. Instead, Family Constellations were an instrument for letting the dead come to us in a dignified way.

In the time when I was still immersed in thoughts about these issues I attended the conference "When Humility Heals and Powerlessness Brings about Peace" in Kassel, Germany in March of 1999. There, to my surprise, I heard Bert Hellinger's voice:

> . . . focus on your center . . . step into your
> center . . . and then go through and beyond
> your center to the realm of the dead. Lie
> down with them . . . quietly . . . look at
> them . . . now slowly, you get up and begin
> looking back to where you came from, and
> look towards the light. Go further up to
> the light, enter your center, let it become
> wide, go through it until you are returning
> to the full daylight . . . your eyes are open-
> ing."

The scientific term *phenomenological systemic* seems to be gaining acceptance when it comes to describing the work that was developed by Bert Hellinger.

Although there are no animal furs, bone oracles, drums or magical masks to be found for miles around and everything occurs in the sober atmosphere of a hotel or therapy room, I am increasingly aware that in our work we "find what works" within the basic configurations of sha-manic healing actions. Could it be any more animistic than in constellations where the symptoms of an illness, the Ego, the Soul, the goal of a business, death, guilt, the farm (the inheritance) . . . are asked how they feel?

It was not long ago that we "modern ones" listened in amazement when we heard Hellinger bring to light ancient love connections, powerful ties, a blind drive toward bal-ance, and the effects of age-old orders as they arose from the depths of the family soul to rule over us today, as if we were archaically obeying magical actions. But we also learned how this blind loyalty and desire for ties could be raised to a higher, conscious level and how destiny, in spite of everything, sometimes does shift to align itself with or-der and with love.

Meanwhile, the instruments with which this can be done were not less amazing, and there are therefore many who regard the constellation as the actual thing itself. We forget that constellations are just a tool, of course a tremendously important one, but lastly nothing but an instrument in a bigger process.

Here, too, we find the ancient charm, compressed rites of passage, and the sensed presence of an undefined good force which works through us, and maybe most surprising of all: dealing with those who are already dead in various interactive ways.

In my Constellation Work I found four archaic healing strategies relating to the dead and our way of dealing with them:

> 1. Just like the old shamans do, we retrieve lost parts of the soul of the patient.

> 2. Just like the old shamans do, we try to bring the relationship between the living and the dead in order.

> 3. Just like the old shamans do, we help the dead to achieve clarity, peace and reconciliation among each other, in the service of the living.

> 4. Just like the old shamans do, we help the dead to achieve clarity, peace and reconciliation among each other and for themselves, in the service of the dead.

In the following sections I examine each of the archaic healing strategies in greater detail.

*But in the future a bridge will be built once again,
consciously, to those who have died.* —Rudolf Steiner[3]

1. The Soul Hunt

It seems as if the orders of love are a common order for the living and the dead, even if we do not know how deeply this applies to the realm of the dead, the great realm.

The first order, which is that nobody who has a right to belong must be excluded, thus applies equally to both the living and the dead.

Shamans endeavored to retrieve lost or stolen parts of the soul from other realities such as the realm of the dead. In order to do this they had to switch over to the other worlds and engage in a dangerous hunt to catch the soul prey. It was only by re-integrating this into the soul of the patient that he/she could become healed (heal = whole).

Within this basic image of shamanic actions we, too, fetch back parts of the larger soul of an extended family that have been lost from conscious memory. These parts usually consist of those who have already died, such as for example stillborn children.

Once all parts are put back into place, the patient feels whole and complete, connected, and with a sense of belonging. He/she is liberated from the task of representing the one who was previously excluded and of expressing his/her absence.

*For those who have passed through death need
and long for the love and the thoughts of those who
were close to them on the earth.* ---Rudolf Steiner[4]

2. Accessing the good power that flows to us from the
dead.

One of the surprising results of Constellation Work is
that there is generally no difference in the effect that the
living and the dead have on the system. They act independently of their status of being and often separate information is needed in order to recognize which representatives
in a constellation represent the dead.

The relationship between the living and the dead, i.e.,
the ancestors, can therefore be cleared up with relative ease
through the processes that have so far been developed in
Constellation Work. Although considerable courage is
sometimes required of us in our work, the shamanic voyage
into other realities seems to be incomparably more dangerous and filled with existential fears and latent horror.

The longing of our soul to fulfill a movement toward
someone that has been interrupted—especially toward the
parents—often shrinks back when the person that our soul
is drawn to is dead, because every connection seems to be
cut off by death. Once the entanglements are solved and
once the constellation has exposed the separation from the
dead as an illusion, the movement can reach its goal, often
with surprisingly little help. We then lie happily in the arms
of our parents, at our mother's breast, just like on the day
we were born. Death cannot truly sever loving bonds.

If an unrecognized attraction pulls us toward the dead
so we are willing to give up our own lives out of an unconscious love that makes us want to be close to our loved
ones, or if our soul's magical striving even wants to save

them from death, then the separation from the realm of the dead is a boundary we must learn to be aware of and respect. There is no problem about going on a trance journey into the realm of the dead, lying down next to the beloved ones, allowing our heartfelt feelings to flow and strengthening our connections to them. But then the journey back to the living begins, taking us across the boundary, strengthened and upright.

The many years of experience with constellations have taught us that the dead appear in full dignity when they are not forgotten and are afforded a sense of belonging, and when their destiny is honored as being theirs. Then this dignity radiates down onto us. We feel the power to stand up straight and a calm composure flows from this secure sense of belonging. The peace of the dead gives rise to a calm presence in us. It would perhaps be rewarding to gather all the beneficial blessings that come from the dead in a book of power.

In special cases, however, such as when the living do not let go of the dead, or when the dead, in their confused state, do not let go of the living, the boundary between the living and the dead becomes a zone of special entanglements.

Neither guilt nor love gives the living the right to hold on to their dead in everyday life. Although it may be illusory, it seems to disturb the process whereby the dead open up to the Great Realm and at the same time it seems to have bad effects on the living. The dead have a right to their death.

In those cases, when someone has taken on a lot of guilt and when the only remaining solution is for him/her to leave the family—such as in the case of a murderer— then not only do the family members have a right to this solution being carried out but so do the perpetrators themselves.

It is only when the door closes behind them and the family can breathe freely that they can remain outside in atonement. Then like Cain after his fratricide, while under the special protection of God, it seems that after some time they reach the gate which leads them to the community with their victims and with the other dead. The length of the road they must travel seems to be relative to the perpetrator's willingness to truly look his/her victim in the eye and to fully become aware of what he/she has done.

In the end the perpetrator and the victim must accept their common destiny, even if they at first oppose each other like enemies. Their joint and relaxed entry into the Great Realm is made easier if the dead finally separate from those with whom they were entangled and turn their heads with a striving spirit toward those who went before them to the realm of the dead giving them a sense of peaceful belonging in that realm.

Those who take their guilt with them and who exonerate the survivors by taking the responsibility for their actions remain at a higher level. The ancestors, whose blessings we receive and honor and who, when they conceived their children, were in the service of life they passed on, were not perpetrators, but fathers and mothers.

Bert Hellinger has expressed the thought that the exclusion of the murderer from the circle of the family, the closing of the door, actually represents a kind of transfer to the realm of the dead, where their victims already are. This seems to me to be an especially helpful concept for those cases where the perpetrator is still alive and maybe even is a very close relative who is present in everyday life.

In my view and based on my observations, going through such a door seems to lead to a kind of in-between realm, to a time of contrition or, as we saw, a realm where an unredeemed soul roams around for a long time. This seems to occur in very severe cases of crime against life and in the absence of contrition and empathy with the victims.

In practice we often find that such guilty persons, if they are still physically alive, in a certain way actually close themselves off from their families and even from life. Yet for many relatives it is confusing to deal practically with this drastic movement of the soul.

The movement of the perpetrators out of the family into the realm of the dead, (symbolically carried out by their representatives in the constellation) transforms the guilty by closing the door behind them and alters our reception. Although still physically alive they become ancestors, belonging to the dead but still walking the earth. We encounter them in their special mode of existence with deep respect.

The Dagara believe that it is . . . the duty of the
Living to heal the ancestors. ---Malidoma Patrice Somé[5]

3. Working to create clarity, peace and reconciliation among the dead as a healing process for the living.

Recently, Albrecht Mahr reported his experiences[6] in solving entanglements between the living and the dead. The entanglements had arisen because someone died in a state of confusion about his/her situation or remained entangled in unsolved bonds and ideas, and this became a burden for the living. Unreconciled or unclear relationships with those who have died, especially with the parents, can apparently have the result that even after life the dead are under the illusion that they can find among the living what they can only find among those who died earlier (for example, parents).

Here, a third type of healing action is demanded of us—one which has central importance in the tradition of shamanic practices. Maybe the most irritating notion is to create clarity, order, peace and reconciliation among and between the dead, in a way that serves the living; to convey to them the consequences of their confusion, and to accompany them for a while on their path so they can reach those for whom their souls are yearning.

In all seriousness, can a problem issue be solved posthumously at the level of the dead in the service of the living?

Surprisingly enough, the answer—at least in my experience—must be: it is truly possible and sometimes it can be done, sometimes not, just as if the persons were still alive. Although we repeatedly see evidence that the dead generally are friendly toward the living, this is definitely not the case for the dead among themselves. It seems that death itself does not solve anything. Here, we catch a glimpse of the importance this work could have as an aid to the dying. It is in no way irrelevant or without consequences for those who remain, with what thoughts we die or if our soul clings to the living as we die.

In constellations, however, one cannot always get the dead to understand. They then force us to find solutions for the living without their help. If, however, a solution can be found among those who once caused the problems, we get the most lasting and the most healing effects.

Of course I, as a practitioner, cannot offer results from methodological research, but I can offer my impression to others for their own observations: solutions that can be achieved at the source of intergenerational entanglements and that have a conciliatory effect on the dead have the most lasting effect on the living.

As far as I know, no studies have been made of the regularity with which constellations have an effect on other, not immediately involved, family members. Sometimes we hear of quite sensational effects, whereas in other cases the constellations seem to radiate very little influence.

Here, too, I would like to offer my impressions for further observation: it is when solutions are found to inter-generational entanglements that began further back in time that the liberating effects spread out the furthest, reaching members of the system who are not immediately part of the Constellation Work.

The order for passing on the effect of good solutions may be the same as those that apply to life itself: those who were born earlier—the parents—give; those who were born later—the children—take.

In practice this would mean the dissemination of the effects of a good solution occurs fairly well at the same generational level, hardly at all backwards or "uphill," but quite excellently and powerfully "downhill." It is quite obvious that when parents clear up things for themselves, these solutions have strong effects on the children, but the opposite is not so much the case. Thinking further along these lines, I feel this speaks for seeking solutions at "high-lying sources" that usually await us in the realm of the dead.

Example of working with a high-lying source:

It is not seldom that a constellation shows a child was foisted onto somebody else, i.e., that the mother entered into a marriage or relationship when she was already pregnant. If this fact is kept secret the man is forced to think he is the father. After birth the child, too, learns that the man was his/her father. In such cases, one's reasoning mind perceives differently than do the souls of all those involved and they are subjected to more or less diffuse feelings that something is not right.

The biological father, who has been excluded, must then be represented in the following generation. This follows from the basic order, which Bert Hellinger has found and which states that everyone who has a right to belong must also receive this place and that the tribal conscience does not allow such an exclusion.

Usually, a child of such lineage is constantly at war with the official father, without knowing why. Such a split perception on the part of the soul and the mind may also have worse effects, such as for example, schizophrenia. The undefined rage of those who have been cheated continues to affect the system, usually through many shifts and variations, and it leads to eruptions of violence. Feelings of guilt and the bond with the earlier partner often keeps the mother at a distance from her cheated partner and encourages incestuous dynamics in the system. These dynamics can sometimes be attempts at creating a balance, whereby the mother practically pushes her son or daughter toward her cheated husband.

Intense results and dynamics become visible, although the three parental parts (the great-grandparents of the client) in the chosen example had long been dead when the constellation was set up. When these dynamics came to light, they resulted in strong reactions on the part of the representatives. The conceiving father was first amazed, then very angry, sad and disappointed. The cheated foster father was also angry, but at the same time he stated that he felt there was something right about it and that something was put into order. The woman was suddenly flooded by feelings of guilt and shame.

It was then possible for the woman to tell the man to his face that she had cheated on him, that she was sorry and that she took on the guilt and the responsibility for the consequences. The reconciliation, which began between her and the man who had been wronged, could be both felt and seen. There followed a series of further interactions between those involved, such as the reunion between the child and its father, an honoring of the great-grandfather by the descendants, the child thanking the foster father, and a confrontational encounter between the mother and the natural father.

This encounter consisted of an admission of the injustice that had been done toward him, i.e., that he had been denied paternity and the right to his child. These interactions led to feelings of redemption that were felt all the way to the grandchildren. Only now could one hope to successfully undertake actions for the living and of course especially for the client that could help dissolve entanglements, such as systemic identifications. Honoring the real great-grandfather then constituted the final chord that had been lingering for a long time.

In practice, if we orient the Constellation Work toward events that lie further back in time, one consequence is that we in part must refrain from striving to have an economy of constellations that states: *constellations are good if they take only a short time and if they only require few representatives.*

During longer constellations the loss of energy certainly may present a difficulty, but if we encounter family secrets it takes time before the system (the ancestors) is willing to provide information, i.e., for the information to rise to the surface in the representatives or through the intuition of the therapist. In my experience, the trial and error method cannot be used indefinitely, for it is like poking around in the dark and thereby losing energy. This is especially true if the method is used by the therapist in order to validate his/her hypotheses.

If the search is guided by the power of the union of souls and their search for solutions, a power that can lead us during the process, then the line of tension in the constellation is strong enough to carry it through over a longer period of time.

The greater soul's search for solutions at the level of entangled ancestors can be blocked or resisted. In other words, the ancestors may hesitate to let things come to light that they, during their lives on earth, successfully kept hidden or veiled or irreconcilably avoided to do.

This can be seen in the form of ambivalent behavior on the part of the client, whose representative may try to confuse or distract, has sudden memory loss, intellectual absences or dull feelings, or else there may be a sudden loss of energy in the constellation. This requires a firm intervention, or else the constellation must be broken off.

Clearly naming the resisting, or rather the protection-oriented situation, can often abruptly take things further. I do, however, feel those involved are fully entitled to have resistance and protection.

Are We Entitled to Interfere in the Issues of Those Born Before us?

Attempts at finding solutions at the level of those who have died raises basic questions that, in addition to the therapeutic and practical dimensions, also have an ethical aspect: do we really have the authority to get involved in the issues of those born before us, especially if we have the intent of changing their state of being, whichever it may be?

This question remains the same even if we regard interactions with the dead from a basically scientific point of view as a resonance phenomenon in Sheldrake's terms.[7] It then remains an intervention into the state of being of the ancestors and an attempt to change it, no matter how honorable our motives may be.

Instead of seeking a general answer, it seems to me there is only one authority in a position to answer this question fully, concretely, and practically—the ancestors themselves.

What is to keep us from going into meditation and in prayer seeking contact with one's own ancestors with the request for protection, support and humility as well as with the dead, whose healing space we are entering when we set up a constellation? We would do this with the request to be allowed to be a guest in this space, in support of one of their own.

If it becomes apparent that the best approach would be to seek a solution at the level of unsolved issues between the dead, I then undertake a large part of this approach publicly in the group.

I usually turn to the person for whom we are seeking a solution, often long before we set up the constellation, and create vibrations of honoring and respect, indicating one's own smallness in front of the ancestors, and I explain to them that the affairs of the ancestors is really no concern of ours.

During all this I try to motivate the persons seeking the solution to find a good inner attitude, without arrogance, with which to approach the ancestors, and to ask for help for healing. I ask them to approach everything without judgment, to treat everything that comes to light with respect, to let go of everything once a solution has been found, and to retain their sense of respect toward the ancestors no matter what may have transpired.

One can thereby avoid a potential therapeutic trap: those who are entangled and who already are seen as "too big" by their parents and those born earlier, can become even more "pompous" by dealing with and trying to change the affairs of the dead, who have a higher position than they.

For me it helps to hold the image of addressing a venerable council of ancestors, whose power is greater than that of the one who is entangled and which has a strong interest in the benefit and continued existence of the family and the tribe. Meanwhile, I suggest to my clients that they enter into a more focused contact with those persons who are expected to be important for the solution, asking them to provide the information that is necessary for their own healing. A good time to do this is before falling asleep the evening before the constellation.

The first permission and help usually comes that very night in the form of a dream or through information that is suddenly just there. It also tends to show up in the form of a decrease in symptoms of resistance and a background energy that can be felt during the work, so that the work seems to happen all by itself.

This type of deepening preparation also provides an orientation for the soul of the therapist and gives responsibility to the greater power. If this is done seriously and in a focused way, with the full weight of our entire person behind it, then I believe the ethical dimension of the work with the dead is well honored.

Such preparations may also help us therapists to fully open ourselves up to the space of emptiness, of "not knowing" and of "not being able to" i.e., taking a phenomenological approach when it comes to how we find direction and wise guidance.

Morphic Resonance and/or Movement of the Soul

The religions of revelation and their secular children, the rational sciences, have made us blind when it comes to immediate perception and fearful when being subjected to a greater reality. The interactive contact with the dead was relegated to the spiritualistic grey zone, but now this possibility has definitely returned into the middle of our lives and is beginning to develop its healing reality.

The post-mechanistic scientific approach that is based on Rupert Sheldrake's concept of Morphic Fields[8] may make it easier for us to accept this, but this is probably done at the expense of the wonderful magic that comes from expanding our realities. However, nobody really knows what a Morphic Field actually is. The field concept is descriptive, and it encompasses perceived patterns of influence that arise at a certain place with a certain intensity. Here, too, reality is ultimately that which has a perceivable effect; it is what we have an effect on and what has an effect on us.

But Sheldrake's point of view, which is based on resonance phenomena, may help us in finding a suitable way of dealing with the irritating fact that the information that we receive in Constellation Work is context-dependent and partial. When processing our holistic perception, which is a striving for meaning and purpose, it is certainly methodologically functional to assume the continued existence of an integral personality after death, but ontologically this would not make sense. One would expect such a person to provide information that is constant to a certain degree.

Yet it is a fact that, when dealing with certain aspects of a solution during different constellations, totally different reactions can occur. Thus on different occasions it seems that we are obviously referring to different states of being of the dead (who are involved in the process). When different family members independently from each other put up the same family segments, it may occur that although basic facts, such as missing siblings, that had been visible before, could be seen again but other aspects were totally different.

Example:

In a constellation, a woman who was a first-born child finds herself entangled in the murder of a child committed by her paternal grandmother. The murdered child could only be calmed down when the grandmother had left through the door and it found its place as a sibling next to the father. When the younger sister set up a constellation a few weeks later, it turned out she was more burdened by the dynamics of the mother line. Her relationship to her paternal grandmother was unproblematic and it was fine to have her in the constellation.

If we imagine the interaction with the dead as constituting morphic resonance,[9] then we only enter into contact with the aspects of the dead that can make something in us vibrate, and corresponding aspects in us that can make the dead vibrate. It is then not possible to make a statement about the state of being of the dead as a live person or, at best, we can say something about a personality aspect that still has an effect on us.

We should, however, not lose sight of the fact that we are dealing with processes and movements of the soul and not with material acts undertaken by persons. It does, to a degree, make sense to assume the existence of the wholeness of an individual soul. "We do not have a soul, we are in a soul." In this statement, which Bert Hellinger often repeats, the individual soul would be something like the subject of the sentence. One could thus also say: As a soul, I am within a greater soul.

It seems that dying is a process of an individual soul that continues after the time of death of the body and that goes through different stages. According to observations, it makes sense to assume that one and the same soul exists in different aspects and in different phases and states. The different subjects of the greater soul can enter into a special contact with each of these aspects. The latest phase of the dying process of such a soul aspect, which has so far been observed with the help of constellations, seems to be the dissolution of and union with (or in) the earlier aspects, maybe encompassing ever larger areas of an ever larger soul. . . .

If there is further corroboration of our observations of the partiality, the context and relationship dependency and the non-simultaneity of soul states after death, then it makes sense to apply a strictly phenomenological approach, and not be tempted to apply the images and information that arise through different former constellation for the same client (on different issues or different aspects of one issue) in a next constellation. For it is the goal of Constellation Work to find concrete good solutions, solutions that are always immediate and apply to the present, and have a good long-term impact. Their impact is in no way dependent on the logical connectivity of partial solutions. Just like the soul, which is disconnected from space and time, appears in seemingly disconnected and contradictory aspects and yet somehow manages to remain one whole, so do the solutions that have an impact on the soul.

*It should also be a sacred day when a soul is released and
returns to its home . . .* ---Black Elk, Oglala Sioux[10]

4. Peace for the Souls of the Dead

The dead, or their unredeemed aspects, appear in dreams in special multifaceted manifestations, for example in order to reclaim the fact that they belong to the system.

I thus recently set up a constellation of a dream, exactly the way it was remembered, and the events in the constellation were dramatically identical to those in the dream. A mentally and physically retarded child of the great-grandparents of the client, an aunt of the mother, was given away for euthanasia during the Third Reich and was then totally erased from the family memory.

There are also cases of apparitions that should not be rashly categorized as pathological delusions. Such apparitions can be tied to certain places, they can be dark and mysterious and sometimes they can be identified as apparitions of dead relatives. It is as if they are seeking something and have a request they cannot transmit directly. Something seems to be blocked, or stuck, and they seek help or in other ways want to make a statement to the family. These souls or aspects of souls clearly have no concept of time.

The last letter from a young man who disappeared during the war had made the mother extremely upset, for it ended with the words: "I am afraid." Because of his size and strength, he was inducted into the Waffen-SS against his will. According to a report by his great-niece to her mother fifty-six years later, upon awakening one morning she saw an apparition in her room of a large man standing there, confusingly real. On hearing this, the mother became very agitated, for the description of the man fit that of her lost uncle. A constellation showed that the uncle wanted to let them know that he was doing fine and that one did not have to worry about him or try to find out more about him. It is my assumption that this message was, in reality, intended for his mother whom he was seeking in the wrong direction—among the living instead of among the dead. His behavior during the constellation suggests that he was alive for a long time after the war without getting in touch, and that the mother may even have died before him.

My personal experiences with finding solutions for the concerns of the dead for themselves, for other dead and for the living are so far very modest, but I think that the experiences will grow rapidly when we begin to pay attention to such processes.

If we continue to bravely face what happens, if we go with the forces instead of wanting to control them, then old shamanic and new phenomenological virtues are at play. They will take us far and will lead us to larger, healing, sacred connections.

The newer developments that could be seen in 1999 in Kassel,[11] San Francisco,[12] and Washington,[13] and that will be seen here at the conference in Wiesloch, Germany provide us with a widening view, starting with the immediate relatives and leading to more distant ancestors, recognizing them as a basic power in our existence.

For all those present it seems to have been a touching and powerful experience when, during his seminar in Kassel, Germany, Bert Hellinger followed Michael Weber's suggestion and created a circle of representatives of female ancestors around a patient who had multiple sclerosis, encircling her lovingly. This circle was itself surrounded protectively by a circle of men. This work had more of the physiognomy of a shamanic healing ritual than of a classical family constellation.

What power could flow through us and impact us if we were to learn even more about how to access these oldest of sources? During the healing process we could enter the memory field of shamanic experiences, we could become fully connected with our ancestors and their knowledge, and we could be connected to the active presence of history. Our lives and our therapeutic activities would then perhaps be characterized by a deeper power, poetry and insight, for this is what appears when we encounter very old knowledge, especially if this knowledge is expressed through our present actions.

In our family constellation experiences we have repeatedly seen that if the grief over the dead has not been expressed then this activates a need to catch up in the next generation. In the tradition of the West African Dagara, this may appear as follows:

> . . . the dead have a right to tears. A spirit, who is not passionately mourned, becomes angry and disappointed, as if his right to a full death had been withheld. . . . Millions of tears are necessary to create a flood that washes the dead into the realm of the ancestors, and to suppress crying would be to do the dead an injustice."
> ---Malidoma Patrice Somé[14]

In these times of approaching ecological crises we begin finally to reassemble that which has been broken and separated. This not only applies to psychotherapy, which is expanding the limits of the individual, but to an ecology slowly beginning to include the human soul and taking form as an interdisciplinary Deep Ecology.

The rediscovery of the connection to the dead and the interaction with them, as it is done in Hellinger's Constellation Work and as shamans have been doing for many tens of thousands of years, goes far beyond the boundaries of deep ecology. It seems to me to be an incredibly important step for human development in our culture, a step whose implications we probably cannot yet see in their entirety.

When the dead, who so far have been so fundamentally separated from the living, unite with them in love, and when the larger soul of the tribe and the family again unites to form a whole, then a great amount of healing energy is released. This energy floods the shores of our goal-oriented actions and affects all those involved in this process. We find ourselves touched by something that suffuses and carries all of existence. Healing becomes a sacred act, sacred like life itself and sacred like the earth. We feel that the dignity of the process of healing, when dealing with the dead, and the dignity of partaking in the community of the ancestors raises us up more and more, making our work at this level into a religious celebration.

All ancient world cultures, whatever local characteristics may have applied, from the Native Americans of the forests to the shamans of the Tropic of Cancer, of Siberia or Hawaii, including our own European ancestors, shared the experience and the knowledge that the world is a whole, living being, a single unified organism, of which the human being is a part. They knew that it does not matter if they are on earth or if they walk in the realm of the dead and that a good connection to the ancestors determines the healthy continued existence of the family, the clan, the tribe, and all human beings.

Religo means to connect back: to connect back to the earth, to the social community, to the ancestors, the clan and the family, to one's own gender and one's own destiny. This is the essential core of shamanic healing and that is exactly the direction that I see our work developing toward—especially after the experiences of this conference. Maybe our rituals for becoming whole will end as they do

for the Sioux Indians, with an ever-deepening   connection
with the words:

Mitakuye Oyasin: All my relations[15]

This essay was first published in the book *Derselbe Wind läßt viele Drachen steigen,* Gunthard Weber, Editor. Heidelberg 2001, 180 pp.

The Return of the Shamans
References and Notes

1. This text was written for those who already have basic knowledge and experiences of Hellinger's Constellation Work.
2. Malidoma Patrice Somé, *Vom Geist Afrikas, Das Leben eines afrikanischen Schamanen*, München, 1996, p.20
3. Rudolf Steiner, *Truth Wrought Words and Other Verses*, Springer V., NY 1979, p. 193
4. Rudolf Steiner, ibid, p. 193
5. Malidoma, ibid, p. 20
6. Albrecht Mahr, *Familienaufstellungen: Wie Lebende und Tote einander heilen können*, working paper, 1999, later printed in: Praxis der Systemaufstelllung, 1.99
7. Rupert Sheldrake, Das Gedächtnis der Natur, Bern, München, Wien, 1992, 143 pp
8. Sheldrake, 1992
9. Sheldrake, 130 pp
10. Black Elk, *The Sacred Pipe, Black Elk's Account of the Seven Rites of the Oglala Sioux,* Univ.of Oklahoma Pr.
11. Workshop with Bert Hellinger, 12.-14.3.99, *Wie Demut heilt und Ohnmacht Frieden stiftet, Kassel*
12. Workshop with Bert Hellinger and Hunter Beaumont, 22.-24.3.99, *The Orders of Love,* San Francisco, CA
13. Workshop with Bert Hellinger and Hunter Beaumont, 26.-28.3.99, *Love's Hidden Symmetry*, Washington, DC
14. Malidoma, ibid, p. 94
15. John Fire Lame Deer, *Tahca Usthe, Medizinmann der Sioux*, München, 1979

2
The Relationship of The Living and The Dead In Systemic Constellation Work

It seems developments and insights come to light more or less simultaneously at different places on earth from different heads, hearts, and souls, as if many people were working together on a common tapestry. When expressed from the experiences of phenomenological Systemic Constellation Work based on Bert Hellinger's principles, one could say that a joint tapestry (a single greater soul) is working through these many people.

In 1999 I was working on my contribution for the international conference on systemic solutions in Wiesloch, Germany[1] entitled "The Return of the Shamans," which dealt with the phenomenon of representation of the dead in constellations and our active interaction with them. At the same time, in his work in Kassel in March of 1999, Bert Hellinger suddenly used shamanically-oriented interventions and, on top of it all, a text by Albrecht Mahr was presented during the same conference, entitled: "How the Living and the Dead Can Heal Each Other."[2]   His text then appeared in the magazine *Praxis der Systemaufstellung* [*The Practice of System Constellations*] and elicited an intense discussion characterized by disapproval. In the following article I am reacting to this discussion with the intention of contributing to creating an atmosphere of clarity and ease.

The critics of Albrecht Mahr's text, no matter how disapproving, pose important questions for myself, and I am sure, for others seriously working with Hellinger's phenomenological therapy.

Thanks to Bert Hellinger's incorruptibility, the interactions with ancestors or with active aspects of the dead, which had been relegated to the spiritualistic grey zones of our culture, have definitely returned to our culture and can now be discussed. No battles of resistance can stop this process; on the contrary, they are good signs of approaching progress.

During twelve years of constellation practice, occurrences and events have constantly taught me to expand my views, especially around the relationship between the living and the dead in the system. This body of experience increased my insight, my knowing, that there must exist a continuity that involves mutual influence. I was surprised to note that my views became more and more aligned with those of pre-Christian healers and shamans.

And yet, even with this view, we need critical rational reflection when trying to reconcile Constellation Work with an (expanded) scientific concept, but only if we are willing to refrain from striking down views that align our perception with words like "hocus pocus."[3]

Rainer Adamaszek is right: we are dealing with the theoretical scientific foundations of our work and we are truly dealing with the *"foundations of our culture."*[4]

At first glance our work brings to light layers of our culture that are much older than those limited by the currently reigning scientific and cultural belief systems. This is the case if we consider the intense rites of passage—the fact that we in constellations interact naturally with representatives of the dead and that we feel the greater power that operates through us in our work, or the magical movements of the soul, such as the drive to follow someone into death. Here we become aware of the archaic physiognomy of cryptic bonding love and its orders, which

26

Hellinger has brought to light, thus baffling our triumphant sense of modernity.

It seems to me that we are not only on the path toward overcoming the false separation between the living and the dead, but also between history and prehistory. Could this not indicate a great step for the healing (heal = whole) of our culture itself?

I am firmly convinced that the restlessness that drives modern man is rooted in a disturbed relationship to the ancestors . . . Only chaos can arise from an unbalanced relationship between the living and the dead ---Malidoma Patrice Somé, African shaman[5]

But in the future a bridge will be built once again, consciously, to those who have died. –Rudolf Steiner[6]

In my presentation, "The Return of the Shamans" (Wiesloch, 1999),[7] I described more in detail the following four archaic healing strategies that I found, relating to the dead in the system, and how we deal with them in Constellation Work:

1. Just like the old shamans do, we retrieve lost parts of the soul of the patient.[8]

2. Just like the old shamans do, we try to bring the relationship between the living and the dead in order.

3. Just like the old shamans do, we help the dead to achieve clarity, peace and reconciliation among each other, in the service of the living.

4. Just like the old shamans do, we help the dead to achieve clarity, peace and recon-

ciliation among each other and for themselves, in the service of the dead.

This list will of course raise the suspicion of our work being esoteric and will cause accusation for having equated work with representatives in a constellation with work with the real dead. In the following passages, I will clarify why it still makes sense to me.

Marianne Osang, in response to Albrecht Mahr's report about his experience of the impacting connections between the living and the dead, stated this "no longer has anything to do . . . with an understandable therapeutic concept."[9]

In one sense she is right, but the question must be asked: whether we should ignore our true experiences in favor of a narrow concept of therapy that has been handed down through tradition, or if we should grow beyond today's scientific views with the experiences gained in Constellation Work in the tradition of Hellinger?

Rainer Adamaszek's statements, for example, make it clear that experiences that have been made during Constellation Work can only be relegated back to the psychoanalytical realm by using brute force.

He writes: "Hellinger's phenomenological method demonstrably . . . makes an invisible reality visible." He warns against esoteric misuse and then he relegates the reality that has been made visible to the realm of the symbolic.[10]

My question is, "Why should this be more valid than to view it esoterically?"

In the meantime, when it comes to fundamental principles used by the therapist, it seems to me neither of these views is relevant.

Let's take a closer look at it. If we are witnessing a reality that becomes visible which hitherto was invisible, for instance, it becomes evident "that a dead person is not aware of being dead and of clinging to an individual or more family members . . . , "[11] we are usually in the midst of a work with a determined healing intention. In that very moment, of such a strange revelation, we don't need any esoteric worldview, nor do we need a psychoanalytical reinterpretation—and we definitely do not need theoretical scientific musings by the therapist. What we need instead is the facilitator's fully open perception. We need his/her full commitment to what was revealed, to the way in which he/she deals with it, and to how it has a liberating and healing effect on all those who appeared through the representatives, including the dead. That means, in such an instant, that we have to drop all beliefs, assumptions, ideologies, 'scientific knowledge', and questions about the so-called objective truth.

It would be totally absurd to welcome good effects which show up for representatives of the living family members in constellations, but reject those that show up for the representatives of the dead. Here, phenomenology encompasses and allows the greater view, whereas psychoanalysis and other therapeutic modalities appear smaller and more constricted.

The element of interpretation, which is so important to psychoanalysis, has little space within the process that occurs between perception and therapeutic action in a constellation. It is not only my experience that the deeper meaning of an action taken by the therapist in this powerful force field of a constellation often does not unfold until after the solution has been found. The therapist, too, is under influences that indicate an expanded reality.

Recently a client's sister, who had been lying in a coma for months at a place far away from the location of the Constellation Work, awoke once their grandmother's murdered children had found their place. This occurred when the grandmother (who had been dead for a long time) in the form of her representative, began to take the consequences of her actions.

Such effects are not the result of any therapeutic concept, but of a much greater process. When we face up to this then our secure worldviews, whether scientific or religious in nature, inevitably start rotating. In my view, the most productive attitude that one can take in the service of a good solution is to abstain from explanations and to accept what happens.

If one speaks of "hocus pocus," one assumes that one knows what is possible and what not. To what extent do such assumptions close us off against what truly occurs?

The religions of revelation and their secular children, the rational sciences, have made us blind when it comes to immediate perception, and fearful when being subjected to a greater reality. How then, are family secrets that often have been kept hidden for generations and that are afterwards confirmed as being true to be explained? How is it possible the appearance of dead family members (whom nobody has heard of) can come to light simply from a client's projections?

Three weeks after one constellation, the photos of two small girls appeared. These were the sisters of the client's grandfather who had died when he was over ninety years old. To the knowledge of all those alive, this constellation set up by the granddaughter was the first time these girls had appeared—and they did so based on signs from the representative of the (dead) grandfather.

Such experiences invalidate the notion that what transpires in constellations is simply a manifest reflection of our inner subjective world and "a piece of theater focused on the private, symptomatic life of a person."[12]

To me there is no doubt that when putting up a constellation, massive processes of projection are involved and these can be seen in various phenomena of resistance. In other cases we often experience evidence of a kind of unconscious knowledge, for example when a sibling who has so far been unknown appears and the sibling who is putting up the constellation says something like: "I always really wanted a big brother" or "Somehow I knew it!"

If we were to remain with the view that the events in a constellation are not only partially but entirely the result of the projections of the clients who are seeking solutions, then the above practical example at least requires the assumption that our inner world must be connected to the inner world of individual members of our system, including the dead, if not to the pool of knowledge of the entire system.

What speaks against the possibility of applying the process, whereby we project contents from the unconscious into the constellation and at the same time we project parts of the hidden knowledge of the system. I am suggesting here that we understand the subconscious of an individual as a hologram, each element containing the whole. In the light of experiences such views, which are related to Jung's concept of the collective unconscious, have been shown to be insufficient if we were to rely exclusively on them.

As all critical contributions have emphasized, our focus must be on the issues of the one seeking solutions. Yet it cannot be denied that constellations have remote effects and elicit changes in behavior among those not present. This occurs without their knowledge of the content of the constellation and without them even knowing that a constellation was set up. So far I cannot see any predictability for such remote effects, but the fact they occur seems to be important to this discussion. This is especially true when, as is normally the case during supervision of Constellation Work, the clients are not present and the supervisor works with the constellation that the supervisor works with the constellation that the therapist sets up on behalf of his/her clients.

In my practice in Germany, I once set up a constellation utilizing cushions for the system of an American woman, who at the time was in the United States. I worked with it by feeling each individual position, and I found that she had to be systemically identified with an earlier wife of her grandfather, who, according to the official version, now lived in Japan in a second marriage with a Japanese woman.

Thereafter, the client told me over the phone that she was feeling better (she could enter into a relationship), but even among distant relatives no factual information could be found indicating the existence of the grandfather's other wife. At the time, the grandfather did not react to her questioning letters, and this was not typical of him. Some time later an author published a biographical book about the grandfather that attested to the existence of a second Japanese wife; the present one was his third wife.

I have never gotten to know this man who has lived in Japan since 1945. I can therefore hardly be seen as being aware of his innermost secrets. The knowledge and the solution became available only through the field of the constellation, through which I moved.

The information that appears in a constellation thus neither emanates from the projections of the person seeking solution, nor does it stem exclusively from the interactions of inner worlds or of a trans-individual subconscious.

The question of how systemic information is transmitted can, at this state of research therefore, not be answered fully.

Hans-Dieter Dicke suggests carrying out a *"rational scientific reasoning around. . . research . . . into the Constellation Work
. . ."*[13]

To carry out such a task in the most beneficial way, I would like to suggest we follow perhaps the most progressive approach we can find here and that is, undoubtedly, the approach of Rupert Sheldrake. His post-mechanical scientific approach to the occurrences, using the concept of the Morphic Field[14] may help us to easier accept that we obviously are somehow communicating with the dead or, to use Sheldrake's language, that we enter into resonance with the memory field of the dead.

The concept of resonance explicitly relates to something that is separate from me as the one who is resonating, but who must exist. I begin to resonate, vibrating like the source from which the excitement emanates.

With her words: "this means to me that I really let them (the dead) be dead . . . ," Marianne Osang makes a point of saying "I am separate from them."[15] In her view, the irrevocability of death and our separation is "trivialized and disguised."

In response I ask; Does letting the dead be dead really mean that I am separated from them in the sense of not being connected to them? But is it not specifically the experience from Constellation Work that a great blessing comes from the perceived connection to the dead?

Of course the dead have to be dead in the physiological sense of the word in order for us to be able to interact and enter into resonance with them. Applying Sheldrake's theory, which has been substantiated through many empirical observations and experiments, to our question "In what way we can enter into communication with the dead?" it seems reasonable to assume that we are not faced with personal beings.

Maybe the knot in the entire debate lies here, for if we follow Sheldrake's logic, we are not immediately connected to the dead person. Morphic Fields and morphic resonance are immaterial, and memory (also among the living) resonates in this field, i.e., in a sense separated from the body, whereas the brain is simply the receiver. The same is true of the gene, which Sheldrake sees as the receiver and not as the carrier of inherited information. The memory field continues to exist after death and even extinct animal species can, it seems, be reactivated. It has already happened that extinct species of trout were hatched from trout eggs that had been subjected to a certain electromagnetic field in the laboratory.[16]

Every form creates such a field and is created in such a field. A swan gets its swan form through the Morphic Field of swans. Analogous to this, this specific form, this constellation of members of a system produces a form field, which contains information about the system. This information is independent of the physical existence or nonexistence of the members, and the representatives in a constellation serve as receivers of this information.

With this background it definitely makes sense to identify the perceptions of the representatives with the represented persons, without claiming that they continue to exist in the body. The dead are, without a doubt, dead, but there is something that we can connect with, something real, that continues to exist.

Maybe the approach taken by Sheldrake's theory, which is based on resonance, may help us find a suitable way of dealing with the irritating fact that the information which we receive in constellations is context-dependent and partial.

When processing our holistic perception, which entails a striving for meaning and purpose, it is certainly methodologically functional to assume the continued existence of an integral personality after death, but ontologically this would not make sense.

First of all, one would expect such a person to provide information that is constant to a certain degree. Yet it is a fact that, when dealing with certain aspects or layers of an entanglement or solutions during different constellations, totally different reactions can occur. It makes sense only if we refer to different states of being of the dead, or seen from another angle, to different time segments or differently developed processes.

When family members—independently from each other—put up the same family segments, basic facts such as missing siblings that had become visible before show themselves again, but often other aspects appear that are totally different.

For example in one constellation a woman, a first-born child, finds herself entangled in the murder of a child committed by her paternal grandmother. The murdered child could only be calmed down when the grandmother had left through the door and the child then found its place as a sibling next to the father. When the younger sister set up a constellation a few weeks later, it appeared quite differently. It turned out this younger sister was more burdened by the dynamics of the mother line. The younger sister's relationship to her paternal grandmother was unproblematic and it was fine to have the grandmother remain in the constellation.

If we picture the interaction with the dead as constituting morphic resonance, then we only enter into contact with the aspects of the dead that can make something in us vibrate, and with corresponding aspects in us that can make them vibrate. Therefore it is not possible by the experiences gathered by constellations to make a statement about the state of being of the dead as an entire person. At best, we can say something about a personality aspect that still has an effect on us.

The theory of Morphic Fields constitutes one possibility that may satisfy our rational side somewhat, considering the outrageousness of operating with information that comes from the dead themselves via the living representatives.

If we, in this way, have accepted the possibility of interacting with aspects of the dead that are still operating, then we are faced with the next difficulty. How is it possible that the actions of the living can influence the dead? As the concept of a memory indicates, the morphic field appears to be of a preserving, conservative nature. This helps us understand why it is difficult for something new to establish itself in the world but much easier to repeat or continue something that is already there.

On the other hand, it is specifically this fact that makes it difficult to understand how (in the received vibrations) the constellations can result in changes in behavior on the part of the dead. However, it is exactly from those changes, as our experiences show over and over again, the living clients receive the most impacting and profound healing impulses, no matter whether we are dealing with a guilt that was repressed in life and that is now taken on, or if we are dealing with a conciliatory "I am sorry" between the (dead) conflicting parties.

Let us assume that during a constellation we are connected, through morphic resonance, to information, personality aspects, unsolved vibrations . . . from members of the system who are not present, i.e., also from the dead, then it follows that these (the souls) obviously have the ability to learn, or put differently, that their fields can be changed posthumously.

It is my impression, and this has become stronger over the last few years, that solutions to issues that were caused through the actions of earlier generations and became the source of later entanglements only succeed if a desire for a solution is inherent in the system itself. In more personal words, those born earlier must want to bring their issues in order, since they could not (fully) do what needed to be done to solve them in life. This means that the memory field also contains the more or less accessible solution, which is a kind of striving for completion, and the therapist and the person putting up the constellation must be open to this solution.

It therefore does make sense to assume that the living can bring things in order for the dead, and that there are solutions that can occur between the dead.

> *The Dagara believe that it is . . . the duty of the*
> *living to heal the ancestors.* —Malidoma Patrice Somé[17]

One of the many surprises encountered when setting up constellations with the dead is that one is confronted with the very many conditions that the dead are in. There are many different ways of being dead, ranging from a soul's restless wanderings or tormented feelings of being unredeemed, to a peaceful passing, just to name a few. These states of being can change drastically in the course of the Constellation Work.

Here, as I see it, we again encounter the limits of an explanatory model for the interaction with the dead, for this phenomenon cannot be satisfactorily explained by the theory of Morphic Fields. For such states of being, or feelings, do not stem from a memory. They are not something historical that is still vibrating, but instead something current that relates to a state of being (or its field). That means the Morphic Field model of understanding, if applied exclusively, also tends to reduce the complexity of what is occurring.

But nobody really knows what a field actually is. The field concept is descriptive, and it encompasses perceived patterns of influence that arise at a certain place, with a specific intensity. Here, too, reality is ultimately that which has a perceivable effect; it is what we have an effect on and what has an effect on us.

Taking care not to go too far, it still seems as if we are communicating with the influencing aspects of the dead, although this cannot be fully explained by the concept of Morphic Fields. It seems to make more sense to speak of a kind of resonance of the souls in various states of being. This description would allow the process to be accepted as real, but at the same time its mysteriousness would remain protected.

In overview we can thus roughly identify four groups of influencing forces in constellations:

> 1. The projection of individual contents of the individual unconscious through clients whose constellations are being dealt with; and/or

> 2. Their projection of trans-individual, unconscious contents (which stem from the other members of the system) according to the principle of the hologram and/or contents of the collective unconscious of the system; and/or

> 3. Morphic resonance, i.e., receiving information by vibrating with the memory or form field of others or with the system as a whole; and/or

> 4. Mysterious soul contact (a process of balance and transmission), which operates (so far) beyond explanatory models.

Although the last group can be suspected of being mystifying, it goes the furthest and points toward what Bert Hellinger, for good reasons, tries to understand in a strictly phenomenological way.

If we abstain from theory and instead, adapt to what appears in front of us through our body, soul—and mind, thus agreeing to a humble empiricism—then we do not need to explain what happens in a constellation. In addition to the orders of love, we do not need to provide any explanation about how something in the system occurs, for example how a systemic identification with someone occurs who lived two generations before me and of whom I have never heard or seen anything.

From the perspective of a consistently phenomenological approach, the question of how the information actually arrives from the dead is almost absurd: yes the information is useful if the person being represented is still alive (providing this can be validated), and no if they are already dead? Constellation Work is rooted in a healthy pragmatism: something appears and is used to create a healing solution, and that's it.

The theoretical debate does not originate from a phenomenological position, or from a lack of something that the work would need in order to improve. It comes from the difficulties that schools of therapy and other cultural bodies have when they cannot avoid the fascination that emanates from the experiences with Constellation Work, and then they try to package them into their own belief structures, which are much too narrow.

Also from a methodological point of view, a strictly phenomenological orientation is recommended as being pragmatic and effective.

The afore -mentioned observations of the partiality, the context and relationship dependency, and the non-simultaneity of soul states after death caution us not to succumb to the temptation of simply taking the images and information that arose in earlier Constellation Work with other issues, and transferring them to new Constellation Work.

One should not lose sight of the fact that we are dealing with the processes and movements of the soul, and not with the material actions of persons (even if systemic entanglements lie at the root of material actions). It is the goal of Constellation Work to find good concrete solutions, and these solutions are always immediate and apply to the present, and they can have a good long-term impact on the future.

Their impact is in no way dependent on the logical connectivity of the partial solutions. Just like the soul, which is disconnected from space and time, appears in seemingly disconnected and contradictory aspects and yet somehow manages to remain one whole, so do the solutions that have an impact on the soul.

Seen systemically, it makes sense to assume the wholeness of an individual soul.

"We do not have a soul, we are in a soul." In this statement, which Bert Hellinger has often repeated, the individual soul would be something like the subject of the sentence. One could thus also say: As a soul, I am within a greater soul.

Based on what can be seen in Constellation Work, it seems that dying is a process of this individual soul, a process which continues after the time of death of the body and which goes through different stages. According to observations, it makes sense to assume that one and the same soul exists in different aspects and in different phases and states. The different subjects of the greater soul can enter into a special contact with each of these aspects. The latest phase of the dying process of such a soul aspect, which has so far been observed with the help of constellations, seems to be the dissolution of and union with (or in) those who have lived before, maybe encompassing ever-larger areas of an ever-larger soul. . . .

Here, systemic work means changing the structure of influence as it appears, according to the potential for change, which is inherent in the structure itself. In this structure all elements that are involved influence each other mutually, independent of their status of existence (living or dead). Expressed in Hellinger's language this means that there is a large area in the common larger soul of a clan or family that lies in the realm of the dead, and a smaller area of existence, which lies in the realm of the living. The entire soul appears as the union that encompasses both forms of existence. In my view, this is as far as one can go in one's statements, without leaving the structure of phenomenological methods or even philosophy.

As long as nothing different appears in the constellations, it should suffice.

This essay was first published in the magazine:
Praxis der Systemaufstellung (Practice of Systemic Constellations) 1/2000, 18 pp

The Relationship of The Living and The Dead
References and Notes

1. *Die Rückkehr der Schamanen, vom Umgang mit dem Tod und den Toten,* in: Gunthard Weber, (Hrsg.): Derselbe Wind lässt viele Drachen steigen, Heidelberg, 2001
2. Albrecht Mahr, *Wie Lebende und Tote einander heilen können,* in Praxis der Systemaufstellung, 1/99
3. Rainer Adamaszek, *Die Unterschiede zwischen den Kulturen...,* Aufstellung 2.99, p. 10
4. 4. ibid.
5. Malidoma Patrice Somé, *Vom Geist Afrikas, Das Leben eines afrikanischen Schamanen,* Mün. 1996, p. 20
6. Rudolf Steiner, *Truth Wrought Words and other Verses,* Springer, NY 1979, p. 193.
7. Heinz Stark, *Die Rückkehr der Schamanen, vom Umgang mit dem Tod und den Toten,* in the book: Derselbe Wind lafst viele Drachen steigen, Gunthard Weber (Editor), Heidelberg 2001, 180 pp.
8. Relating to the larger soul of clan and family, for example in the form of stillborn children.
9. Marianne Osang, *Systemaufstellung oder Mystifikation?,* Aufstellung 2.99, p.9
10. Adamaszek, p.11
11. ibid., p.12
12. ibid., p.11
13. Hans-Dieter Dicke, ... esoteriknaher Tonfall..., Constellation, 2.99, p.82
14. Rupert Sheldrake, *Das Gedächtnis der Natur,* 1992, (the concept of resonance. 142 pp)
15. Osang, p. 11, 12
16. Kerner, D. and J., Der Ruf der Rose, Köln, 1992, 94pp.
17. Somé, p.20

3
The Art of Family Constellation:
Conceptual Thoughts About
High Quality Training

Inflationary tendencies

In 1995, when I began introducing Bert Hellinger's Constellation Work in America, hardly anyone had ever heard about it. Those were difficult beginnings. The psychological marketplace was supersaturated with seminars, and the Constellation Work offered a blunt and sometimes brutally honest experience with an air of confrontation, and a seemingly directive method. Not very sales-oriented in the American style. On first glimpse, my work was often taken as German rudeness.

Added to the above, Constellation Work provoked, offending a fundamental American conviction and belief in engineering. This conviction, that life and the state of the world and even fate is something that is, in principle, subject to a kind of engineering. There is the deep belief that everything will work if you do it the right way.

In spite of this fundamental constructivism, people slowly started to realize the healing effects of the Constellation Work. Within a short period of time, I was confronted with the fact that therapists wished to be trained in this work but also that moneymakers in the psychological market (and more or less dubious people) tried to grasp their chance. They attended workshops and asked many questions.

After paving the road, Bert Hellinger himself came to the States, others came, and the adaptation of Constellation Work for the American market began.

The things that happened left me stunned. For example, there was a psychotherapist who attended two weekend workshops—tapping into the fog of the dynamics of his own family system—who then declared publicly that I had trained him. He started to work as a trainer himself.

After many years of experience with this kind of adoption of Systemic Constellation Work, attending a few workshops and declaring oneself a trainer, I concluded that this way of learning, in most cases, is inappropriate. It cannot reach the depths necessary for this work to unfold its full force. This fast food approach to training keeps you, and the work, on a superficial level; a grab-and-go acquisition of pure know-how leading directly to a saleable product (decorated by a sugar crust to guarantee a smoother selling) is, above all, often combined with all kinds of "spiritual" shallowness.

In the face of this development, some hold the mystifying idea that the work will protect itself, or that there is nothing you can do, which is also a comment on this cheap development.[1]

To resign in the face of the spirit of the time and board a flying carpet of pure commerce does not suit our work. The character of this work is opposed to the governing spirit of the time. This prevailing attitude has gone so far as to accuse Hellinger and our work of preaching chauvinist conservatism.

For all real connoisseurs of Constellation Work, this view is complete nonsense. We are dealing indeed with a striking archaic deep structure which is derived solely from observations, empirically repeatable, but in no way with ideological concepts.

When, finally, I could no longer stand to observe inactively these inflationary developments—which, unfortunately also included established therapists and professionals of related fields—I took the initiative to offer a formal training program in Systemic Constellation Work. At the time, this offering seemed to me a breach of taboo against formal training. However, my intention was to do what I possibly could to establish well-trained facilitators in the market so, in the long run, the chaff would naturally be separated from the wheat. The offered training program demanded continuity for an extended period of time, and an intense engagement with the work—and oneself.

Each trainee is confronted with his/her own psychological attitudes towards life and survival strategies, belief systems, and (cultural) ideologies, and has to answer the question, what should better be dropped. By exploring and participating in the phenomenon of resistance, it is inevitable that our own character, shadows, and blind spots are touched. It becomes obvious that the real immersion into the Phenomenological Systemic Constellation Work demands more than most people are, at first, ready to give.

The ever-growing offering of constellation seminars by facilitators who, in increasing numbers travel to America, continues in the mode of a workshopping concept of training and disregards high-quality education based on long-term training. Under these circumstances it felt wonderful to read the following in a request for more information about my extended training program: *"I am especially interested in the quality of your training. Since I realized as a participant the intense effects of the work, so that I feel that the training has to develop a deep sense of responsibility and it requires respect to do the work."*

Thoughts About The Training (education) of Artistic Personalities

I strongly argue that all of us who teach Systemic Constellation Work need to critically examine our offerings, to ask whether we show the courage to demand something of the students which opposes the common logic of the market or not. Our orientation, hereby, should be the question: are our offerings—in structure, content, and method—able to teach graduates who, afterwards, will forward and further develop the work in an authentic manner?

Berthold Ulsamer published a good book on this topic. Translation of the German title reads, "The Craft Side of Family Constellation Work." In this book, he argues that only the craft side of family constellation is teachable and learnable—but not the art and the depth of the work.[2]

This is an attitude, however, that provokes a contradiction in myself as an artist.[3] I feel this education, which is occupied with nothing less than the working with the good order of the soul of families and clans (and the systemic forces in organizations and businesses), it is more than appropriate to create training processes that go beyond the craft side and follow the ambitious aim to develop a process which promotes the art of constellation. This is to say the education should help the trainees to find their own paths, to become teachers who find creative turns in the work without losing the authenticity of the work, rather than someone who simply applies reproduction, copying the work of another.

When we use the terms *art* or *artist*, we are generally not looking at the huge number of artists or corresponding excellent artwork that goes mostly unnoticed by the public. We look at outstanding persons like Michelangelo, e.g., who was an unhappy person for all his life but succeeded in welding craft and art in an unsurpassable way, and who chiseled the new view of the world of the Renaissance from marble. When we look at his work, we have to believe that beyond an immense industriousness, and the simple link to the spirit of the time, somehow a bestowed genius had to be working. But why do we assume this could happen only to a very few people? The myth of the few divinely-gifted was welcomed mostly by those forces that secretly controlled the cultural, historical, and social processes of selection—who decided what kind of art was presented to the public.

The experience that something greater is working through us simple mortals is lively among us facilitators. Matthias Varga von Kibed described this experience of Constellation Work in a nice way:

> We are, when we register this knowledge or this insight or this experience, guided to see that this knowledge is on the one hand truly our knowledge, but in that way, as if it was just given to us as a gift. This leads us to acknowledge this in a different kind of way, with a feeling of gratitude and receiving a gift, not just of having solved a mathematical task or riddle.[4]

When I was completely absorbed by Constellation Work, this is exactly how it feels; that exactly the same energies are mobilized and spent as when I was in the middle of creating artwork.

At the end of a seminar, when I look around at the circle and see the relaxed faces, the eyes lighted by life, when I feel how the room inside of me, and around me, is filled with gratitude, I often have to think of Joseph Beuys and his notion of the social artwork. It is a pity that this great artist of the 20th century did not live to get to know

Constellation Work. I think it would have given his striving for art as a social sculpture a whole new dimension.[5]

The term sculpture is newly defined by Beuys, with regard to being synonymous with art in general, even with man himself.[6]

Beuys withdrew the art from *"the few genius artists"*[7] and assigned it back to the people. His famous words, that everybody is an artist, does not exclude the genius, it socializes it.

Genius does not only mean creator but, in the Roman antiquity, also guardian spirit or divine embodiment of the essence of a person, a community, or a place. In the light of systemic experience we nowadays call this kind of genius, related to the natural sciences, less spiritually but more technically "a field."

This peculiar field that takes us into its service and gifts us, despite the social expansion of the notion of art, needs the artistic subject, the celebrating shaman, the magician of the constellation forces, the realizing, transforming and purposeful mediator. Beuys himself is here an example. He never left his so-called "Fluxus Happenings" to the audience.[8] His composure was integrating and touching, but he clearly represented the gravitational center of the event, exactly as we know it from Bert Hellinger.

When we describe people as artists, we usually have in mind the kind of people who are able to absorb wider realities and collect and concentrate them through their personality, and express them by finding adequate forms. To answer our questions of how to learn and how to teach and support the growth of this artistic productive capacity, we have to focus on personality—artistic personality. Whatever it is in an artistic personally that is set and stimulated by such an educational process, that then leads beyond the simple reproduction of the adapted, it is in no case something learned solely for the functional. It is something that belongs to the molding shape of the whole personality, and

48

certainly it belongs to educating and growing. Personality is capable of change.[9]

The personality is, in the end, the only passage through which the artwork and art of Constellation Work can take shape (and in taking shape, it is already shaping the artist).

Therefore every serious education, in my opinion, essentially reforms the personality, in spite of the question of whether the teachers in this process are aware of it or not.

As a long-term teacher in the arts in different fields beyond public schools, I realized that there are hidden individual aesthetic potentials in all learners. Why should this be different for the mental and psychological resources with regards to the art of Family Constellation, re: Systemic Constellation Work?

These hidden potentials are found where the qualities are stored which had been refused in the process of socialization, in the material that has successfully withstood obstinate attempts at elimination or repression. If we are capable of setting these initial impulses to open and encourage the trainees' potentials, we will witness beautiful movement towards unfolding and growing unique artistic personalities.

Those impulses and openers are, of course, of a different nature than the kind of interventions and teachings needed for the process of acquiring the technical aspects of the work.

They are rather comparable with interventions in a humanistic therapy for advanced clients.

The Position of Craft in the Training

Craft skills are connected to the use of the tools. The choice of tools is related to the material you work on, and the good use of such tools is something you have to learn well.

All craft-related subjects and tools should be gathered together in a training program. These include all elements of phenomenological-systemic therapy: its ethic attitudes, empirical experiences so far acquired, methods, experiments, basics of phenomenological philosophy, paradoxical and systemic thinking, the ability for complex and instantaneous perception. The catalogue of needed craft skills comprises far more than the implementation of the "orders of love," or the techniques of Constellation Work.

Craft skills have always been a fundamental aspect of the artist's syllabus. It was a productive paradox that this was the case even in the age of modern art, which at the same time, is deeply biased against all craft. In spite of the sometimes conflicting nature of the relationship between art and craft, the historical separation of art and craft took place. In constellation art we have to balance both aspects in a most productive way.

If it is true, that a facilitator is then good at his work when he is able to *"adapt flexibly to different situations,"*[10] the question should be permitted, where and how does he acquire these skills? What will I as a teacher do, for example, with a student with a rigid character, a notorious applier of rules? How can I help the one or the other to strengthen trust, to expose themselves composedly to the void of (completely uncrafty) the space of not knowing and inability, the fundamental attitude of phenomenological perception?

If craft were enough for an education, there would be indeed something like a *right* and *predictable* constellation, because it is the core of craft to know how something is rightly and well done.

But as we all know, this is not a part of Constellation Work (or art). It is the essence of a successful artwork of our days to overcome the categories of right and wrong. Even the inappropriate might become a critical expression of an important context, or the incentive to take a major step out of entanglement. Equally important, a mistake on the craft level can sometimes suddenly lead to, or create, a surprisingly releasing effect.

Three Reasons Why It Is Not Enough Anymore to Acquire Only the Craft of Constellation Work

Experienced facilitators of the first generation, who acquired the art of Constellation Work more or less on their own, may ask themselves if it is necessary at all to think so deeply about teaching and learning and concepts of training, facing a subject that itself unfolds in the work so wonderfully.

In my opinion, there are (at least) three weighty reasons why it is no longer enough to acquire the craft in this way, and why this acquisition of both craft and art should take place in a structured and thorough process of education.

1. Second and third generation facilitators enter the scene

An artistic "constellator" personality, already educated, is only in need of new material and tools of the trade it will change and grow with doing the work.[11]

I have the impression that something shifts in the demand for education in phenomenological Systemic Constellation Work. Younger people, who naturally have less experience in life, push into the work. They come from different fields. The reservoir of extensively (therapeutic) experienced, educated and knowing "psychonauts" is decreasing. Either the work swallowed them, or they are moving toward retirement.

At the congress at Wiesloch, Germany in 1999, Albrecht Mahr, from the depth of his experience in Constellation Work, sketched in his speech his ideas about the requirements someone should have before entering Constellation Work. Two statements I remember as exceptionally impressive: the candidates should already have a therapeutic qualification and, in addition, should not be younger than fifty years.

Because I fulfilled these requirements, it was not difficult for me to nod and applaud. But I applauded also because I know from the experience of many years of doing Constellation Work, how demanding this work is.

The younger people who are fascinated by the work and feel a calling to do it, will not be content to wait until they are fifty and then come back.

There must be a way to awaken something inside them—something that is fifty, probably fifty thousand years old—a feeling for what composure, sincerity, courage and steadfastness ask from you, and deepest trust into the active forces. We have to further their courage to go to the edge with respect and a sense of responsibility, and to encounter the realities that appear.

There must be a way to communicate the insight that healing Constellation Work is only possible with powerful modesty, even humility. We should awaken our boldness to submit to the process with the risk of defeat, to experience acts against one's own ego, to renounce ownership and originality of healing and solution and, last but not least, to renounce the curious desire for knowing and the usurping personal power from the powerful event.

2. The Work Demands Artistic Skills

On the platform of the above (what we've just mentioned), connoisseurs of the work may easily understand the necessity to invest thinking into profound learning processes. This necessity is dictated by the force of the work itself.

This force is able to hurl us high or into great depths, like a gigantic Pacific wave full of thundering life and great danger grabs a man on a surfboard. It demands we adapt our personal balancing power to the greater happening so as to easily escape the danger held by the destroying forces. Ability here is a synonym for trust in one's own skills, for devotion to the greater forces that bear us.

To reach this high art, it is not enough to paddle in shallow water. The virtues we need, we can only develop in serious practice—they can't be trained, or bought. The qualification for work at the borders[12] demands enough time for growth, continuity, exchange of experience and good trainers.

3. Systemic Constellation Work is in Permanent Change

Systemic Constellation Work is in a highly dynamic state. Compared to what existed at its beginning, it has become more complex and differentiated. This dynamic state also demands we watch the needed qualifications closely. We are only at the beginning; no year passes without new insights, reflections, discoveries. We are trusted with the development of a very young art that asks from all who form it, and are formed by it, to become researchers, discoverers and developers.

The required abilities and qualities are not easily picked up or gained by "workshopping."

We must risk creative intervention with the spirit of discovery on the one hand, and experimenting only with deepest self-discipline, respect, and sense of responsibility on the other. From the harmony of personality and process, the feeling for balanced acting comes.

About the Qualification of Facilitators of Systemic Constellation Work

Bert Hellinger himself was, of course, sometimes a great example for a facilitator who represented the above qualities and made them significant for his method. But when I look at all that he has uttered so far about the theory and teachability of his work it seems to me he neglected, or failed to recognize, this essential part. Where would his work be without these virtues? Without them, how could his work achieve so powerfully; how could he be so terribly strict, so loving, so completely effective?

Of course we cannot all become Hellinger and educate our character in terms of years of training—or could we? To become a little bit of the early Hellinger should not do us any damage, I think. The mimetic learning helped me to feel clarity, courage, dignity and power within myself and, through this, mobilize my own respective potentials. People who are embedded in the process of Hellinger's soul work, and who face its depth, are unavoidably charged with a force of personal growth, and assigned the task of engaging themselves in developing their own character and personality.

Before I accept a person for training, it is important for me to ask whether the person is in tune with me, and my way of working, or not. That's why I ask trainees to participate in two or three of my workshops before beginning their own training.

I do so since the concordance of trainee and trainer is basic for the success of mimetic learning. Mimetic learning is a mimicking learning conduct that does not only imitate, but in which the trainee also *identifies* with the way the trainer does his work. For a while the trainee virtually incorporates this person, or becomes this person in the relevant aspects.

Incorporating the conduct of the trainer charged with personal qualities effective to the therapeutic process brings similar personal aptitudes in resonance with those potentials of the trainee. Thus the trainer's qualities and powers are felt as one's own, and it is possible that using these qualities and powers will be amplified and felt by the trainee as one's own. This way effectiveness and functional power can be proved and experienced right away in practical work.

The special qualification of the trainers here is to permit, or allow, these mimetic processes and, at the same time, counterpart them. Help for building identification comes from the excellence of the work of the trainer who, as a practitioner, is a model. Help for building unidentification comes from revealing insecurities, difficulties of the trainer, from telling unsolved questions, marking personal restrictions, by participating in events held by other facilitators (as part of the training concept), and especially from naming and encouraging the recognition and use of the particular personal abilities of the trainees, which are different from the trainer's.

In addition to mimetic learning, tracking down, appreciating, and supporting those special—and perhaps unrealized or unappreciated—potentials is the second centerpiece of my design of training in Constellation-Art Work. Especially in this aspect, we must see if trainers are simply good facilitators—or also good teachers, a distinction that, in the artistic field, rarely happens. We find there a strange blindness to the simple fact that a good artist is not synonymous with a good teacher of his/her art. We should avoid this blindness in our field.

Not long ago, I read an advertisement for a constellation training program that claimed the facilitator had already done more than a thousand constellations and therefore now had enough experience to become a trainer.

I would have liked to have read that, beyond that, he also had many years of experience in other disciplines of humanistic therapy, preferably in those that deal with character transformation, or at least profound experience in adult education.

I feel the prerequisites, professionalism and age, that Albrecht Mahr demanded in his speech should at least be a common basis for trainers.

The ability of the trainers to realize the potentials of the trainees leads to more effective development of the trainees, even when those potentials differ from the specific qualities of the trainer. To try to somehow double the model is not the way to bring out the special personal qualities and potentials. They can only be nourished from the trainee's living personality.

The potentials of a trainee, of which we are talking here, contain not only the hidden but also the character obstacle that shows itself on the road to becoming an artistic facilitator of Constellation Work. Mostly, several difficult and delicate personal operations are necessary before this is realized and accepted, and before it can be changed into a resource.

There are many indications that systemic entanglements have essential influence on the process of forming an individual character or support the development of certain character types. (See essay, *The Embodied Family System.*) Continuous training provides the opportunity to touch these deeper layers by dealing with relevant dynamics and forces, and in return, the gain is made of specific process-oriented abilities. We usually find those where trainees have their "blind spots."

For example, once after several training sessions had passed, one trainee had noticeable difficulties in understanding the modus operandi with guilt as Hellinger found it. Since this phenomenon showed again and again, I proposed a constellation. Because the phenomenon differed clearly from the other conduct, it had the character of a symptom. What we found was a heavy dynamic of guilt in the generation of the parents that was completely hidden.

When an inner solution of such an entanglement is allowed to grow, it can give the personality of the facilitator a special competence. In the above example, a special skill for guilt dynamics may develop here—he/she will practically "smell them."

These "blind spots" in facilitators that can be changed into useful qualities, can also, if never uncovered, become a permanent obstacle for solutions and a source for development of resistance.

About Duration and The Structure of the Training

There is no doubt that the above-sketched processes can't unfold in a "crash course" but need time to mature and a longer relationship with a trainer may be necessary. Otherwise, a favorable process of mimetic learning, the time needed for change and growth of characteristic obstacles or systemic "blind spots" to unfold, is not possible.

Such a concept has to include practical experience and supervision after a short time of basic learning and, beyond that, experiences with other facilitators. This should take place without interrupting the continuity of the training group and the initially elected trainer. The external experience and their retrospective effects can be reflected together this way.

The shortest possible duration of a high quality basic training, in my opinion, should be at least two years. This includes a preliminary phase (getting to know the trainer), and then the training itself with an introductory phase and a longer study phase. Together this should amount to at least six seminars of six days, and additionally, several self-organized study groups in between training seminars. A better concept though, might be forty to fifty days of seminars in various forms and formats (current training in the U.S. consists of forty-nine days).

The inner structure of such a training effort should give the trainees as much creative space as possible and as much support and orientation as necessary. It should also provide a complex offering of practical experience.

The following principles of learning should be effective in it:

1. Exemplary Learning

The training should include seminars in which the trainers not only work with trainees but also with regular clients. Thus it is possible to get experience with a greater number of themes and cases, with people of different languages and ways of processing the world (different ethnic groups) , with the whole spectrum of clients. Additionally, this gives the greatest prospect for the trainees to get into resonance with the hidden, the *forbidden* entanglements in their own systems. In this sense, "forbidden" entanglements means blind spots created by systemic resistance/taboos. Long after entanglements that lie in a more conscious layer of the soul are solved in a good way, such resonance phenomena leads to deeper layers of dynamics when it reappears in certain aspects in the work of other clients.

2. Mimetic Learning

This way of learning leads to the adaptation of fundamental qualities such as courage, trust, dignity, and incorruptibility as described above, since these are a vital aspect of phenomenological Systemic Constellation Work.

3. Practical Learning

Constellations to resolve real issues in the circle of the trainees, in which they facilitate constellations with other trainees as clients, usually encourages further practical attempts in other environments. Above that, they help the trainers to realize specific potentials of the personality of the new facilitators; they also help to find what kind of supporting measures are needed.

4. Body-centered Learning

Perception is a central category of phenomenological Systemic Constellation Work. Its first-rate instrument is the body.

Dealing with the body language of clients and representatives, informative use, reinforcement or surmounting of presented (emotional) postures, movements as well as breath and muscular restrictions, succeeds best if the body of the facilitator knows these postures itself or he/she is able to immediately empathize with them.

The body serves as a differentiated and differentiating organ for the Constellation Work, to distinguish one's own emotions and bodily perceptions from those that are induced by the field. Moreover, it serves the perception of one's own bodily reactions to clients; it serves conscious resonance to vibrations one picks up; it serves to feel the atmosphere and energy level of the group; and last but not least, to empathize with the effect of sentences of power.

5. Problem and Solution-oriented Social Learning

This is, I feel, an important part of the training. There has to be space for the discussion about insecurities, for questioning unclear method, fuzzy theoretical basics, and ideologies. There must also be space to question the conduct of the facilitator—and also for the possibility to reach agreement about what can be sustaining, solid, and supportive. It was conspicuous how much grumbling, confusion, criticism, and lack of clarity could often be heard in the breaks of Hellinger's big events and afterwards, but how little space was given or taken during the event to discuss these things. I recognized during the last conference in Wuerzburg, Germany (which even had the term "Conflicting Fields" in its title), a climate of this kind of silent abdication.

In training we are not receivers of a doctrine of salvation but students of an exciting new way of thinking and experiencing life. Training means wrestling with doubts and awe, insights and rising up of newly occurring questions; it means a space to examine disparities of observations and exceptions to orders or rules.

6. Research Learning

Trainees should, individually or in study groups, comprehend and present basic experiences, background and systemic possibilities of intervention about special topics (guilt and atonement, adoption, death and dying . . .) from literature (including audio visual documentation) and notes of their own practical experience. From this they should develop open questions and tasks for further research. Experience shows this leads to a deeper understanding of the contents. Another topic here could be research about other therapeutic theories in relation to the Phenomenological Systemic Work.

7. Direct Practice Learning

Learning in such a training process should not principally be in the way of a preparatory course, though. That means it should not just work through curricula and syllabus that aim towards a later usability. Discussions, questions, and topics should have a place in life, should be rooted in direct practice, and every day's professional experiences should follow what really affects us . . . should follow the "movements of the soul" in the moment.

In general, these thoughts should not be understood as a recommendation for organizing the training as a mere schooling or a pedagogical approach. Rather, we understand the training is similar to the Constellation Work itself—it is not enough to trust one's intuition. If we trust solely that intuition, we are in danger of becoming structureless and arbitrary. On the firm ground of structured knowledge, we can face the phenomenon that immediately appears without losing sight of the demands of the whole training.

8. Operative Learning

The best space for learning is the real space. The trainees should, after a period of adapting the basics, start to work with constellations outside of the training seminars, in their own responsibility, with real issues of real clients. This is the place where they can act, reflect, learn the interface of phenomenological presence and adaptation of structural knowledge. The training group must also, besides other tasks, become a supporting peer group in order to grow into a supervision group.

These peer-supervision gatherings can be useful long after ending the training to support the professional needs among colleagues.

From the above, one might get the impression that I favor a training as a sort of long-term therapy. It is true that I think in an intense training therapeutic elements are inevitable and even wanted, but I built in structural elements to prevent their overflowing. The organization of my training as a system of modules brings an ever-changing arrangement with guest-participants in the training seminars. They provide interesting cases fitting to the study group topics and put, by their presence, a break on overflowing group dynamic processes.

The notion that intense training in phenomenological Systemic Constellation Work is the ultimate short-term therapy is true for that part of the work that is therapeutic. Part of this effectiveness as a short-term therapy is due to the fact that after a solution has flared up, the constellation process is concluded on a high energy level. No unnecessary words, integrating attempts, discussions or other therapeutic measures interfere with this cut. The pictures and experiences of solution or new perspectives are referred back to the deeper unconscious layers of the soul in order to work on in its own beneficial ways. The facilitator retreats in that moment.

A more continuous contact with the same people seems at first to be contrary to this attitude. But the regular contact with trainees for a longer period shows me instead, as also does the periodical return of clients and, in the end, my own history of Constellation Work, that entanglements are of complex nature, and often there are many layers of them.

The necessary thing to do here is to leave those segments that have already found a solution alone, so that the effect can work on them, and to still continue to work on the strained segments nevertheless. This demands sensitive acting, and it can become an aspect of learning in the training, an element on the road to the art of constellation. On this platform, it should be clear that the trainers also should have a place where they can continue to work as part of their own system.

The old saying that we can only accompany the clients as far as we ourselves could go is also true in systemic correlations.

This essay was first published in the magazine,
*Praxix der Systemausfstellung (Practice of Systemic
Constellations),* 1/2002, 6 pp

The Art of Family Constellation
References and Notes

1. Such mystifications are, as it seems, a common thing among people who give themselves a spiritual air. Instead of facing a problem, you can hear things like, *In this case I have to question the field* that means, constellation is used like divination. At the genuine side of the scene, maybe also with Bert Hellinger himself, I get the impression that through the *movement of the soul* and the concept of the always bigger soul, the all-regulating God might be on his way to be introduced again and the strictly phenomenological approach could be in danger to become a theological one.

2. Berthold Ulsamer: *The Craft Side Of Family Constellation Work,* (Translation by Heinz Stark from German, title: *Das Handwerk des Familienstellens),* München 2001, S.15: *The art and the depth are not learnable, the craft is. The few geniuses, who conquer new territories, should not forget the great number of craftsmen.* The later English issue of the book took on my suggestion to consider Constellation Work an Art!

3. For seven years I studied art at The Art Academy and learned fine arts, which I later taught for many years.

4. Matthias Varga von Kibed: *How We Invite Actions To Manifest Within Us Through Constellation Work,* in: Weber (pub.): *The Same Wind Lifts Many Kites, (Der selbe Wind lässt viele Drachen steigen),* Heidelberg 2001, S.43

5. Joseph Beuys: *But the priorities are clear. Art in the social field is the farthest possible development so far, in my opinion.* Interview, 1981, Götz Adriani u.a., Beuys, Köln, S.366

6. Sculpture as an all-enclosing intention, encroaching the genuine notion of the genre, is understood as a process of becoming aware, which results from an imagination that releases certain forces, and which condenses in thought and action, in shapes, in pictures, in language and so forth.
7. Ibid., S.110.
8. This was the case with the Happenings in America, but not with Beuys' Fluxus Happenings.
9. If I idealistically believed that an artistic gift somehow falls down from the sky, I would never have had the courage to enroll at a fine arts academy. Undoubtedly, there are more or less advantageous assumptions with which someone starts such an education. In my experience, such assumptions prove in the long run mostly as prejudices, that cannot withstand in the face of what artistic work really demands. It is therefore no surprise that, especially in the artistic fields, we realize that the support of the artistic personality is in many ways subject to teaching and learning efforts as way to further the development of an individualistic artistic concept, complete withan individual artistic language, or personal handwriting.
10. Ulsamer, ibid, S. 1
11. In teaching I experienced all arts students that came from crafts (arts and crafts skills or special schools of design) to be in great difficulties. Their firm stand in knowledge, practiced know-how and application (of rules) was shaken. People who practiced therapy as a respectable craft are beginners in the art of Constellation Work. It demands completely different things from them. I remember how much of my well-known stock in

Reichian Body Therapies, Gestalt and Arts Therapy I had to abandon, when I started to trust in the phenomenological Systemic Constellation Work.

12. *Working at the borders*, is a term introduced by Bert Hellinger at various lectures; it refers to a basic mode of operation in Systemic Constellation Work. Since interventions in a constellation process are often serving the request for an underlying hidden dynamic, therefore they have a researching, experimenting character, they are probes, so to speak. That means when we do a search we are used to going to the extreme, to the edge, or to *the borders*. We are exploring first the worst possibility in order to find dynamics, and proceed further by going backwards if necessary, persuing the question of what else is here possible, and what would make sense in the lay out of incongruent information? For example: one might find a dynamic in which it is obvious that a system got stuck and representations are happening in later generations involving our client with a deceased member of the system. The system also shows signs of guilt, of an atonement through the behavior and life performance of the client. We would try out whether there was a homocide behind. But are there still signs of incongruency of phenomenons which are indicating: yes there was something like that but not exactly, that we are oriented to something less dramatic but with partly similar *effects*. One might finally find there was an accident and the surviving members of the system were carrying a lot of guilt, or above it all sombody involved accused another person of the system to be a perpetrator or at least the cause of the accident. That kind of behavior usually happens

instead of surrendering to the fate and the unavoidable pains of mourning and grieving. This way of working requires from a facilitator a lot of skills, sensibility and courage.

4
Family Constellation On the Reservation

Reservations as places of preservation

American Indians are under much notice here in Germany, as we can guess from the tremendous amount of Indian literature on the book market. When kept in the romantic notion of the "good savage," these survivors of the genocide of the Native Americans appear to be witnesses of a continuous harmony of man and nature, and with the wholeness of cosmos.

However, if we acknowledge the reality and look closely at the conditions and circumstances in modern Indian life in America, we have to suspect that we project onto the Indians what we are lacking and longing for. That we are searching for strong images contrary to our technical civilization should not be too surprising if we look at the extent of deprivation in which we live, besides all wealth, uprooted in solitude and estranged from nature.

To the European modern age it seems we can manipulate nature endlessly, turn it into an object of exploitation by industrial production, or bring it down to just green scenery, a backdrop, in order to commercialize it. Even the woeful remains of the wilderness in remote areas have become commercial objects of the tourism industry. In this view, it would appear that free nature itself was put onto reservations, the big remains subjugated all over the globe, held in check with heavy machinery and chemical weapons.

Our inner nature, its archaic soul, our part of the organism earth as a creature, also suffers the same fate: exploited by industrial utilization, held together by chemotherapy, and straightened out in the permanent bombardment of psychologically-armed media offensives. In this onslaught, our heart and mind cry out for protecting spaces.

Reservations (that held in reserve) had, and increasingly have, an important significance for our deepest layers of being living creatures; something can be protected there that cannot find a place elsewhere in the overwhelming utilization-culture anymore.

Perhaps the futuristic society in Aldous Huxley's *Brave New World*, published in 1932,[1] seems less far in the future these days with genetic reproduction accomplished mainly by cloning. Huxley foresaw a society where the meaning of a highly conspiratorial term *could only maintain itself* in a reservation where people succeeded at least in some aspects to live in an imperfect but humane way. This highly conspiratorial term is the word "mother."

Reservations, in my opinion, are highly meaningful for a qualitative creation of the future. Be they for nature or philosophy and arts[2] in the middle of the industrial mainstream, or to offer areas in which tribal societies may survive, reservations enclose something like the archimedic point[3] of the historical moment.[4]

The fact that the cultural and social history of the American Indians has been handed down to us we owe not least of all to the establishment of a reservation system. This system has helped to pass on tradition until some elements could be written down accurately. This history is now available, not only to us, but also for the Native Americans themselves.

Even if the American Indian reservations appear to be places of poverty and death—they also support a kind of defiant survival. Even filtered through double translation, the words of Indian wisdom succeed in stimulating the vibration of power and beauty of creation within us.

In awe of creation we find ourselves, shrunken to humble size, as simple creatures among others, looking at our sister the grasshopper with astonished respect . . . listening to the speech of the stone . . . . Chilled in the morning glow, enfolded in the warmth of the whole, we can feel something of its essence in the shining of the light in the dewdrops.

Sensual, immediate power of language—schooled by millenniums of oral records—offers a perfect poetry and joy of reality that directly serves life and helps us to become aware of our nature-bound existence. It acknowledges every being, weaving and appearing singularly, thus enfolding preciousness, reverence, worship, time . . . and frees us, when we listen to it, from the "European prison of thought."[5] Testimonies from American Indian wise men and what remains of the deep relationship Indians have with the earth, when held up in contrast, show the European arrogance, ignorance and destructive violence against both foreign cultures—and our own as well. In these long-held traditions, we feel the treasures that may have vanished from our own history.[6] Here, I think, we find the reason why, especially in Germany, there is so much interest in the culture of pre-Columbian Northern America. It is an interest that goes far beyond Hollywood.

We are completely isolated from our pre-Christian, shaman tribal culture, a culture that was terminated with the genocide of the church against wise and healing women, the so-called witch-hunt. We became separated us from our roots and from those who somehow still had a relationship to the nature religions of the pagans. The romantic idealization of all Teutonic inheritance of the 19th century destroyed the rest and, if any at all remained, the exploitation and distortion of German heritage by the Nazis completed its devastation.

Thus the indigenous cultures on the reservations of America preserved at least words and feelings like that of "Mother Earth," words that resonate in us with the old oblivion of our own history. If we interpret the signs rightly, the longing for a life in harmony with the greater whole is becoming a mighty stream nowadays. This expresses itself in the ecological movement and its philosophical reflexes such as the Depth Ecology,[7] the development of complementary holistic medicine and psychotherapy, the new thinking of philosophy[8] and, in a great way, with Systemic Constellation Work.

Family Constellations—Reservations of the Soul

The constellation of family systems unfold their elementary
Powers because they speak with pre-verbal images
and because they unite in a rite of passage past, ending and new
orientation in a highly concentrated realm of time.[9]
---Gunthard Weber, 1993

The phenomenological work with Family Constellations binds us generally to archaic aspirations of the soul that are effective within us for a long time. They let us see how thin the layer of the Enlightenment is, and how little influence segments of civilization have in the soul. In the depth of the soul the movements of life rather show as defined by subconscious love for attachment, which expresses itself in magical sacrifice of health and life in service for the blood bond, in perpetual mutual effect of the living and the dead, in an enduring contact with the ancestors.[10]

With Hellinger's work we therefore not only return to personal roots in our clans and families, but we also are immersed in early human history that has been ruled out, but which still secretly has an effect on us. We realize basic elements of our bio-social stock and learn to use them on a higher level (of conscious love) at the same time.

In the special time-space of a constellation, linear time is abolished and past, present and future coincide, magic can show, change its powers, merge into a good flow of life.

This happens in the preserving realm of the soul, our inner reservation and that of the greater soul of family, clan, and community of ancestors, in which we are always contained beyond our life at the surface.

Family constellation seminars always serve the healthy continuum of such human reservations.

Temporary Reservations as a Realm of Experience

For many years in my interdisciplinary practice, I have offered (and still do) seminars, which I call Re-rooting seminars. These are apart from the regular Systemic Constellation Work that I do.

Re-rooting seminars help to find our roots again in the body, the gender, the clan, family and community of ancestors; in profession, nature, in the great soul, the world as a whole.

In these seminars, Constellation Work serves the retro tying (religio) in the broadest sense. The "Movements of the Soul" and Family Constellation are the center of the gathering of various viewpoints and their tools, such as body therapies, work with artistic media, meditation, and last but not least, experience in and with nature.

In these seminars, generally held in powerful places in nature, have a quality of initiation; strong elements of indigenous tribal culture, especially of the North American Indians, play an emphasized role.

I borrow from their simple, earth and life-woven spirituality that is active in everyday life, in which everything in nature is animated and "wakan"[11] and whose highest spiritual creative and effective power is called "Wakan Tanka"[12] which means "the great secret."

This harmonizes wonderfully with the deep insights of our phenomenological work, and for the time of the Re-rooting seminars, both accompany us.

In this creation of a reservation for an actually-extinguished tribe, the timelessness of the soul reigns despite our being surrounded by a busy civilization.

On the Way to Pine Ridge

In light of my Re-rooting work, you will understand how much I appreciated having the chance to do Constellation Work on an original Indian reservation among real tribal Indians.

In 1996, when I started to introduce phenomenological Systemic Constellation Work in America, I could not foresee that four years later I would have the opportunity to become immersed in the reality of an Indian reservation; the Pine Ridge Lakota Reservation in South Dakota.

I brought three qualities that helped my work on the reservation. First, although I came from far away I knew (from long studies) about important personalities of the Lakota nation and of their culture, including details of old rituals, which undoubtedly gave me a bonus of trust. Second, as a German I was not an immediate part of the white American society, so I was not under suspicion of being a descendant of the perpetrators of the genocide. Third, I am an immediate descendant of the perpetrator generation of genocide, those responsible for the Holocaust, and in this area especially qualified by the work of Bert Hellinger.

Additionally, Constellation Work with Americans whose families in recent history were entangled with the conquest and settlement of the west showed me the ambivalent character of American historical experience up to now.

One constellation I did, for example, was with a woman of about forty years who had built a successful business on the reservation, working herself to exhaustion to help her Lakota husband and his clan create a livelihood. She did not realize her entanglement with her grandfather, who had immigrated from Europe and settled on reservation land which was good farm land and had been given to white homesteaders by the U. S. government.

This grandfather stole the horses of the Indians, changed their branding and thus built up a livelihood for his family.[13]

The descendants of the frontiersmen and homesteaders are in a grave conflict of loyalty. Seen by the eyes of the second half of the 20th century, they realize themselves as descendants of conquistadors, invaders, and perpetrators of genocide. Maybe every single person does not feel it so deeply, but they are at least affected and tormented in their conscience.

At the same time, these people are rightfully filled with admiration, thankfulness, and pride, and urged to honor the pioneer's achievements, fully recognizing the indescribable hardships of their ancestors.

In this dilemma they often react with repression or defiance and prefer to stick with racist variations in which Indians are completely denied their status as human beings.

This imperialist component continues also in official acts even now in a more or less hidden way, evident in the continuing missionary work of Christian churches, various integration programs, and various measures taken by the government.

The term "boarding school" evokes memories of children ripped from their families, clans, tribes, and all traditional ties and tortured in the name of civilization. This memory is still present in all older inhabitants of the reservation. Full of helpless pain, rage and desperation, they are not able to look away from what was done to them at the boarding schools.

One Constellation Work showed, in addition to that of the children, the suffering of the priests who, as their teachers, were hated by the children and were used by church and state to further the act of cultural destruction and breaking of innermost bonds. This constellation had a conciliatory effect; the Indian woman who acted in this way could now turn towards the future.

Lakota Reality: the Reservation as a Realm of life and Suffering

After a workshop at Rapid City, South Dakota, I surprisingly got an invitation to visit Pine Ridge Reservation, including an extended interview at the KILI FM,[14] the reservation radio station. The interview was followed by an event in the gym in Kyle, South Dakota to demonstrate the Systemic Constellation Work.[15]

Deeply stirred by the sudden fulfillment of an old and heartfelt wish, I wanted to concentrate before the interview, and started to climb up a steep hill close to the radio station.

Far—incredibly far—I could see over the ocean of grass from horizon to horizon, in the gigantic cloud-piling sky. What an idea it had to have been, to go west in a wagon, traveling through this trail-less land! I breathed in the sweet scent of the prairie. It was wonderful, soothing. The expanse before me heightened and became a time of watching, breathing, watching.

From the southeast, I watched shapes coming up from the glare of the noon heat. A group of people emerged, walking through the high, hard grass towards the hill. Of course I realized that I saw a figment and looked to all sides, turned away, tried to get rid of the picture, but as soon as my eyes turned into the old direction, I saw the group was still there. They came closer fast, and I recognized they were a group of men, haggard, starved . . . no doubt they are from Wounded Knee.[14] The old man in front lifted both his hands and said clearly, without words, "You have to help us here!" Torn between rational doubt and being overwhelmed by what was happening, I promised to do my best. Only after the interview, while I was sitting in the car, did I realize that it was not the descendants of the survivors of Wounded Knee who still lived here who had asked for my help, but the dead of Wounded Knee, the ancestors . . . . What help do these dead need, I wondered, and with whom else but the living should this help start?

The living; forgotten are the old paths, forgotten and hidden in disease, diabetes above all, and alcoholism, malnutrition . . . captured in bitterness, criminality, poverty. Their own language has almost been lost—only few people still know it.[17] The men are broken warriors with toothless pride, bearing the trouble and the survival of the tribes; strong women, still mighty Grandmothers,[18] mothers of fourteen children—seven of them died—seven they could pull through, look at the surviving sons who father new children, ill of alcohol abuse and entangled in violent acts. They look at daughters who had four abortions—the first husband ran away, the second was shot, the third is a good-for-nothing . . . . The tribal community is torn into factions: inhabitants of the reservation, those not living on the reservation, those on different, separated reservations; ethnic subgroups; landowners and landless people; respected and not respected clans; various, partly competitive administrations and agencies; multiple Christian and religious confessions; separate traditional branches who are each trying to reactivate their own culture and are in ideological dispute.

The bad conscience of the more sensitive part of white America leads to various attempts at reparation, apparent in a flood of various help programs brought to the reservations. The inhabitants turn more and more into welfare and therapy "junkies," addicts who will lose in this situation by all means—especially if they take the help that is offered. They are in danger of losing their dignity and their independence and, above all, the few remnants of their own culture.

Already, in light of all this, the demand made by the ancestors of those who were at Wounded Knee turned out to be difficult for me. To look after the many troubles of the soul on the reservation by offering the experience of the Constellation Work? What would the people think? Would they ask, "Family constellation? Another aid program? What does this white man want here, what are his hidden motivations . . . taking money? A medicine man does not do anything like this, and we don't have any money, we don't just take gifts from strangers, really . . . bad experience . . . in history . . . still today . . . .

However, nobody said this aloud.

The vote of "no confidence" was given with the feet. The number of visitors at the demonstration events was small, despite the radio broadcast and the many good words of those who from their own experience strongly advised others to take part. Most who attended were members of a clan who experienced solution off the reservation. But what is the status of this clan? What do the priests, preachers, therapists, counselors, social workers, medicine men, grandmothers, traditionalists say?

Constellation Experiences at Pine Ridge Lakota Reservation

Responding to the call for help was not easy. Four demonstrations, personal introductory tours, many telephone calls and two radio interviews were necessary to finally give me enough people to perform a full workshop. But the preliminary events were very important to gather experience and get to know specific problems that may appear in the work with Indian people at the reservation.

Already in the first work on the reservation, a barrier appeared outside the usual way of Constellation Work. Among reservation people, there was an obvious and ruling code of behavior; *you should not show feelings to strangers.*

Imagine a representative in a constellation with crossed arms and an inscrutable face. Asked how she feels, she answers, "What do you want me to feel?" The accompaniment to this is braying laughter from the circle or participants.

Intuitively I do the right thing and just go on with the same stoical expression, depending on my observation, and on information that comes to me from the field of the constellation.

The aspect of social control was a hindrance for the work at the reservation. Although the reservation's inhabitants are widely spread, it works as a small village where everyone knows everyone, and gossip spreads easily. Later we[10] moved the events to the outside, beyond the boundaries of the reservation, but close enough to be reached comfortably.

The plan to solve entanglements within the indigenous tribal culture was confronted by other difficulties as well. It turned out that many participants were blood-related, or were connected by the tribal adoption system that expands blood relationship. When during a Constellation Work I chose a brother and an uncle, people started to smile.

"Actually, I am her uncle," or "Actually, I am her brother," was the comment. It was very difficult to find representatives who were not related.

Initially, with my American organizers Jamie and Milt,[19] we chose not to "invade" the reservation with strangers, but with the tight social controls, we changed this thinking. In a later workshop,[20] we brought ten people in from all over the U.S. who did outstanding service as representatives for Indian family dynamics. At the end of the workshop, one Lakota woman participant from the reservation said that three days earlier she could not even imagine touching a white person, and now she even embraced some of them. *It is unbelievable what we can do together with white folks," she said.* The experience was healing for both Indian and White, perhaps an indicator for possible future solutions.

Another obstacle to the work on the reservation was the presence of persons in authority who might feel conscientious and loyal about the reputation of dead family members, and thus for the reputation of the clan.

For example, during one constellation the representative of one man swayed and looked completely confused. When I placed a representative for his father behind him, the swaying became worse. As a try, I placed a different 'father' behind him, and suddenly the representative could stand solidly and looked straight ahead with clear eyes. The representative of the mother of the man remarked that this was the right thing.

Before I had the chance to see if the obvious could hold further examination, the elder of the clan jumped up and protested. The mother was his aunt, he said, *"I know this woman, she was a strong Catholic, it is completely impossible."* The group froze; there was no way of ignoring this intervention. I guided the attention to the fact that just minutes ago one constellation was happily released and virtually

78

celebrated, and now, that a result seemed possible that does not fit in, the same method should suddenly fail? Fortunately, the client was vehemently in favor of continuing the constellation—the dawning solution, rather than shocking him, made sense to him. The chief of the clan left the room for this constellation and thus enabled it to continue. When he returned with a knowing smile, we already had found a good solution.

Other real obstacles were to be found in language. The Indian language tradition is concrete and full of images. The German use of semantically open nouns such as "the depth" would immediately cause American English-speaking people to question its use. "The depth of what?" For people coming from the Lakota language tradition, although still English-speaking, such terms as "the depth" would prove ineffective or even provoke resistance

In German, the term "soul," for example, has a widespread meaning and in fact means something that can not be grasped, but still evokes a somehow resonating comprehension in people of our cultural realm. In the understanding of the Lakota, the "soul" means something very concrete. To them the soul is something of the dead that can suddenly jump on you and do you harm on the prairie. On the other hand, "soul" is connected to visionary experience, which cannot come from the simple constellation of representatives.   Instead, they seek this experience only from the pain of a Sundance (a ritual trance experience), total fasting during the vision quest, or in the heat of sweat lodge rituals.

Facilitators in Europe often experience the fact that what happens during a Constellation Work somehow attacks our whole (rational) understanding of the world. For those among the Lakota who turn toward their own traditions after a long period of lethargy, the ease with which mental connections show in the constellation might be reason for rejection, because it can be experienced as an attack on the valued tradition that establishes identity. The good solution often is accepted with gratitude and amazement, but sometimes later there is a startled 'yes-but'. A conflict of loyalty arises which is, above all, also a conflict of cultural identity and thus goes far beyond rejection after a constellation caused by child-like loyalty as we know it from our cultural background.

The explanation of the medicine man for a long history of distress in a participant's family was totally different from the dynamic that showed up in the constellation. The medicine man said, "Your great-grandfather was a white man who did wrong, that is the reason for the distress of the family." This kind of explanation has, of course, another effect towards a solution as we have found it. After the discovery of a dynamic of guilt and exclusion of a killed child, we could offer relief by reintegrating the little soul into the community of the family and referring the guilt to the responsible person.

But there was conflict of loyalty shadowing this solution. Whom should the client now follow, the medicine man or our healing suggestion?

When we would look at the whole picture here, it is not at all to be excluded that a further dynamic might appear in a next constellation that hints towards the medicine man's insights about the grandfather. You never know which actual aspect of a complex weaving you are tapping into during a moment of constellation.

Remarkable, I think, are the parallels of both the medicine man's and the facilitator's efforts towards a solution in this example—both are looking for systemic, intergenerational dynamics. Unfortunately I am not yet knowledgeable about what kind of solutions to intergenerational issues medicine people have to offer.

en in looking back on these intensive days I can still
ith speechless amazement, the depth and range of
e did.

uring the conference I worked with the "normal"
ics of American participants; with descendants of
ust victims, Irish immigrants whose ancestors were
led in the Irish civil war, Russian immigrants whose
drama reached back to the revolution, descendants
ish rebels who fought against the German occupa-
nd I worked over and over again with severe Indian
—with souls, frozen into what seemed to be an
l now," coming from the past. The simple mention-
"Wounded Knee" provokes tears in some Lakota
, as if "the terrible" happened just now . . . .
here were good solutions, and much congealed
ess gave way to new movement.
Descendants of the perpetrators of what happened at
ded Knee turned out to be sufferers themselves.
eople of other nations also suffered. The massacre at
ded Knee sits deeply in the bones of the Lakota, but
only one massacre among many in the world. There
the Holocaust, the same pain, the same hypnotized
g at it, looking away, not really being able to see it—
nting to—bound to the suffering of the ancestors
ur own suffering.
fter this experience I understand even better what
man in the vision on the hill next to the radio sta-
anted. Also that Systemic Constellation Work is a
t way to achieve what the ancestors of Wounded
are longing for; peace in death, harmony with the
e of the living for the dead and that, from the fate
uffered, there should never again come new suffer-

or a moment we experienced what really could be,
l reservation as a realm of the evolution of new life.

But the fundamental similarity of an intergenerational
view makes it possible that the movements of the soul in
Constellation Work are experienced and accepted as "one's
own", as related to deep, old Indian wisdom. During the
workshop at Kyle,[21] a participant from the reservation said,
"*We always knew what you are practicing here with us, we just forgot
it.*"

In general, it seems the traditional conception of the
world of the Lakota is sometimes in amazing correspon-
dence with the experiences we have during Constellation
Work. You don't have to wonder about the fact that representatives of tiny fetuses in constellations have evolved
feelings resulting from their disposal if you assume, as the
Lakota do, that the "spirits" of the children come to us
from the realm of the ancestors and, with procreation, begin to manifest themselves.

In my experience, it was extremely helpful to fit Constellation Work into the spiritual and cultural sphere of the
Lakota nation. We invited open-minded Indians who were
respected in the tribal society as men and women familiar
with tradition to function as spiritual models.[22] They came
at the beginning of the workshop to purify the circle of the
participants with ritual burning of incense and prayers, and
to entrust our healing plan to the spirits and the ancestors.
Every day of the seminar started and ended this way.

Likewise, translating events in metaphors of the Lakota language surely had a deepening effect and caused a
mutual deepening of the day's events. For example, the
expression 'hollow bone' is sort of an equivalent to Hellinger's 'empty center.' In the state of becoming a 'hollow
bone something else, spirit perhaps, may enter us or pass
through us. The facilitator too, must become a *hollow bone*
as well as the representative in the constellation. Expressed
this way, every Lakota can easily understand the happening.

The Wounded Knee Project

After five events in Lakota country, a first conclusion was the insight that phenomenological Systemic Constellation Work in the tradition of Bert Hellinger is perfectly suited to help the healing of people on the reservation, furthering relationships in Lakota families and enhancing the future of the children. The work could lend an immense contribution to the future of the tribe. My impression is that despite sad accounts regarding life expectancy, health and desolate economical and cultural conditions, the Lakota nation is full of vitality. But it is imprisoned in entanglements of an unsolved past and misguided to blind, self-destructive discharging.

The question is: What could be a realistic perspective for the spreading of Constellation Work there?

Because of a generous donation of an American woman, we were able to charge only a small fee to men and women of the reservation to participate without hurting the mental balancing mechanism of giving and taking.[23] This principle could be applied also to attendance in a training of Indians in Systemic Constellation Work, if there were enough donations, and qualified trainees on the side of the indigenous population. Doubtless, this would be the best choice to integrate the work into the tribal life—to train Indian facilitators.

This plan we named "The Wounded Knee Project".

As a beginning we planned a four-day conference we called "Wounded Knee—Wounded Soul." We wanted to reach the following goals:

1. Contribute to the peace of the murdered ancestors at Wounded Knee and their descendants.

2. To encourage the acc own history (of suffering give a basis to a positive or future.

3. To introduce the work tional and spiritual person kota nation, whose suppor project.

4. To make possible an e deep problems of urban I of the reservation, as well further interests and p among the Lakota people.

5. To offer a realm of ex work with unsolved eleme history to American train Constellation Work.

6. To create a broader ser frame of reverence for the the Indians by including va migration groups, and by their protracted historical er

7. To find sponsors and Wounded Knee Project.

8. To find qualified Lakota interested in training and le tate Systemic Constellation

The event took place at Rap November 9-13, 2000.

Maybe it was one of those silent historical moments in which, unnoticed by the greater public, through a somehow heliotropic movement, something new begins.

At this point, at the end of this wonderful, tremendous event, when this insight wanted to become mutual, it came back—the counter-wave, the resistance against reconciliation, the sudden insight that it could have an end with being the victim, with finding identity in suffering. It would also set an end to the wonderful revenge against the white man, the constant "Look what you've done, how badly off we are."

I think in that moment I have made one of the most flaming speeches of my life. Standing up, I felt the ancestors of Wounded Knee step behind me . . . . Well, I don't know if this speech had any helpful effect, but after all I trust, as ever, the good solutions we found in the constellations.

This essay was first published in German in the book: *Conflicting Fields—Knowing Fields, Systemic Constellations in the Work for Peace and Reconciliation.* Editor, Albrecht Mahr.

Family Constellation On the Reservation
References and Notes

1. Huxley, Aldous: *Brave New World*, London 1932
2. I am sure that it would make sense to work artistically with the tableau nowadays, in the middle of globally spread electronic media. The tableau is a medium of the middle ages that does not pre-determine certain ways of reception, has no dictation of time, moreover it invites contemplation.
3. Archimedic Point: The term is derived from Archimedes famous sentence: "Give me a point where I can step on to and I will move the earth." Archimedes expresses his need for a solid point from where he can explore, explain understand and move things (he was not only the worlds greatest mathematician he was also a big constructor). He was longing for a point beyond all the floating relativity. I am also referring here to the German philosopher Walter Benjamin who described revolution (historical progress / f.i. French Revolution = Democracy) as something for that you need points of references outside of your actual system of reality. (Like the French Revolution thought it were the comeback of the Roman Republic). One can show Marx's ideas and ideals of living in communism were taken from the noble knights and their virtues.
4. Benjamin, Walter: *über den Begriff der Geschichte, in: Illuminationen,* Frankfurt/M, 1980 (About the Notion of History)
5. Müller, Werner, *Indianische Welterfahrung,* Stuttgart 1992 (Indian Experience of the World)
6. Metzner, Ralph: *Der Brunnen der Erinnerung, von den mythologischen Wurzeln unserer Kultur,* Braunschweig 1994 (The Well of Memory, About the Mythological Roots of Our Culture).

7. La Chapelle, Dolores: *Earth Wisdom,* Silverton, Co., USA 1978
8. Sloterdijk, Peter: Sphären, Frankfurt/M 1998 (Spheres)
9. Weber, Gunthard (pub.): *Zweierlei Glück, die systemische Therapie* Bert Hellingers, Heidelberg 1993 (English issue: *Love's Hidden Symmetry*, Phoenix, AZ, USA)
10. See the essays in this book: The Return of the Shamans and The Relationship of the Living and Dead ...
11. The Lakota term "wakan" seems closest to the term holy, if we regard the old relationship as it still shows in the English terms whole, heal, holy.
12. The Lakota term 'Wakan Tanka" is often translated as "The Great Spirit".
13. It is to note that such criminal behavior in the new homeland often was the echo of similar events in the original country, maybe by other relatives, and that it was increased by emigration.
14. Interview on KILI FM Radio - The voice of the Lakota nation: *The Secret Blueprints of Fate, their Discovery and Healing.* The interview is available on audiocassette and can also be downloaded as an audiofile from the website www.Starkinstitute.com
15. Also (see footnote no.14) a second interview is available in which one woman with whom we worked intensely that evening, some months later talks about the effect, the work had on her.
16. Synonym for the massacre of a group of starved Miniconjou Sioux at Wounded Knee Creek, lead by Chief Big Foot (half brother of the before murdered Chief Sitting Bull) on their way to Pine Ridge by the 7th Calvary on Dec. 29th, 1890. There were about 300 victims, men, women and children.
17. The Lakota (Sioux) who participated in the Hollywood movie "Dances with Wolves" had to take part in a language course in Lakota, to appear authentically in

the movie. The Lakota medicine man Lame Deer Jr. told us at a workshop in Bremen, Germany, that he wants to make a movie about his father, the famous medicine man Lame Deer (Archibald Fire), in order to show his people their own culture.

18. It is said that the famous Chief Sitting Bull once re-marked that, as a warrior, he has no fear of anyone-- except his grandmother.

19. Milt is an enrolled member of the Cheyenne River Sioux Tribe.

20. The workshop took place at Lakota Fund Building at Kyle, June 14-16, 2000

21. Pine Ridge Lakota Reservation, South Dakota, July 2000

22. Sundancers, healers, medicine people, sweat lodge chiefs.

23. People with financial need still had to pay the sum of $50.

5
The Embodied Family System
Observations and Reflections on the Development of a Systemic Character Theory

In phenomenological Systemic Constellation Work, according to the principles of Bert Hellinger, the body is involved in various ways—so varied that a detailed description of the different aspects would fill many books.

Fortunately, there are already some important texts regarding body-related issues. Here, I would like to emphasize the collection of various discourses and reports from the workshop conference entitled "Verkörperung" ("Embodiment")] which was held in Wiesloch in the year 2000.[1]

The lecture by Friedrich Ingwersens was very revealing to me. It focused on how aspects of body-focused therapy were included by Bert Hellinger himself in his development of Constellation Work.[2]

Both Constellation Work itself and its relationship to body therapy and systemic-phenomenological work have up to now been deepened further and expanded.[3] In this sense, all aspects and current considerations reflect the "state of the art" and provide perspectives for further individual research in daily practice. I would like the following presentation to be seen as a contribution in this sense. It deals with hunches, assumptions, perceptions, and experiences that can serve as impulses and possibly a way of structuring one's own perceptions.

Regarding Bodily Appearance as a Systemic Phenomenon

In the practice of family constellations, we observe how the expression and posture change, often abruptly, once the solution has been found.

The face and the body relax and the toes sink to the ground (grounding). There is a straightening movement, a burden seems to be lifted from the shoulders, the chest expands and if the body is inflated, it deflates. There is a sense of peace and calm, and the person begins to shine. . .

If finding an appropriate place in the constellation of the family and the clan (and thus also a good order with one's own soul) produces distinguishable effects on the bodily posture, the reverse is also true. The entanglements and being locked into certain system dynamics requires certain psychological attitudes that can express themselves bodily and probably even become ingrained, i.e., become a manifest, physical part of a person's character structure.

Seen in this way, every constellation seminar is a practical experiment regarding the systemic phenomenology of the body. If we truly take this perspective we notice, even before anything has been systematized, that in addition to all kinds of body language hints, already the simple bodily appearance can provide us with initial information about the person's type of systemic integration.

If reading the body were thus not relegated only to body-oriented therapies, for which "body reading" represents a genuine diagnostic tool, but if this type of reading were practiced in a systemic context, then we facilitators would have gained the use of an interesting diagnostic tool, too.

I am convinced that many facilitators, especially those who have come to constellations from body therapies, have for a long time more or less consciously been picking up bodily information regarding form, posture and energy, and establish connecting lines to systemic dynamics in their own bodily feelings and thinking.

The question arises: Is it possible to systematize such connections and develop at least tentative hypotheses that first of all relate to hidden family dynamics?

Note that I am not speaking of systematizing such things as "free associations," which arise in us if we are in a phenomenological way open when allowing the appearance of a person to have an impact on us. Such associations or perceptions, for example: "Oh, he really gives the impression of being a concentration camp prisoner," which are strongly colored by the receiver, can probably not be systematized. Rather, I am thinking in terms of character types, such as those that were developed by Wilhelm Reich and his successors. An example would be the so-called schizoid character type, which holds many bodily characteristics that were caused by an early trauma, fragmentation, autistic tendencies, etc. This raises the question: "What could this appearance mean in terms of the systemic background?"

Thoughts Regarding the Development of a Systemically Expanded Character Typology

Wilhelm Reich, a medical doctor and a student of Freud, expanded psychoanalysis to encompass body psychotherapy ("Vegeto-therapy") based on his philosophical-materialistic orientation. In his book, "Character Analysis"[4] he developed as a foundation for his Vegeto-Therapy a body-oriented character theory. As one of its constituencies, he structured his clinical observations regarding the oneness of body and psyche in different types of physical appearances.

Character structures appear as embodied psychological, energetic and emotional patterns of survival. They arise due to specific influences by the parents or other important role models on the development of the child at various age levels (psychoanalytic phase model).

The physical patterns of reaction in a body that have not yet been formed fully[5] are manifesting themselves in various ways, and yet they are created by limited means. We discover processes of splitting off in the brain or variations of chronic muscle contractions, or else impulses to move and take action are held back, redirected or dammed up reflexively, leading to energetic blocks, psychological barriers and stereotypical behavior.

It is almost impossible to assume that systemic dynamics are not involved in the creation of such somatomorphic structures.

Within the framework of this essay I will limit myself to just a few aspects to illustrate the basic types, as they are differentiated by the successors to Reich. The types that are described undergo different kinds of intermingling, yet they can and should merely serve as signposts and not as a possibly stigmatizing cataloguing of human beings.

In my experience an intensive study of this topic is very rewarding and provides us facilitators with at least four benefits:

> 1. At a glance we can recognize our clients' basic survival and assertion patterns and what type of approach and what style of encounter promises the most success and the least amount of resistance against the solution.

> 2. We recognize our own programs and can work to transform them, and at the same time seek to find connecting lines to our own system dynamics.

3. One can thus avoid a clash between a client's very detrimental patterns of behavior and my own. One can for example imagine what would happen if a facilitator who has a survival pattern that is characterized by striving for power (Type Psychopath I) meets a client with a similar pattern and how their communication would play out under the stress of threatening changes.

4. We gain added diagnostic structural aids, which is what we were seeking.

When drafting a systemic characterology that is based on observations from family constellations, we find not only Reich's and his successors' psychological observations but also the observable emotional-bodily phenomena can be seen as manifestations of constant expositions of a certain position within the "form field" (Sheldrake) of the family and the tribe. In other words, the character structures arise from the position of a child in the joint space where forces of the soul (bonding, separation, balance) are operating.

A physical analogy to such an exposition in the form field of the family would be the influence of the earth's magnetic field on a body of iron, such as a ship. Based on its position in relation to the lines of the earth's magnetic field and their local intensity, a magnetic field is induced in the ship and so-called elementary magnets align within it. The body of iron becomes itself increasingly magnetic and, depending on how long the impact lasts, a permanent, semi-permanent or temporary magnetism is generated in it. If such a systemic exposition is truly, in part, responsible for the creation of character structures, this would, so to speak, correspond to permanent magnetism, which is a structure that does not change without something being done to it.

The question is, of course, if it is even possible to build a bridge between a structure that was developed in an individualistically-oriented psychology school (psychoanalysis) to a point of view that perceives the individual in the overall structure of his/her (family) system.

Here, Ron Kurtz' school comes to our aid. In Hakomi therapy, Kurtz uses the bodily character typology that is based on Reich, he abstracts them and integrates them in his information model.[6, 7] In this way he succeeds in integrating four somatically-oriented character types (metabolism types, cortical control, somatic types according to Sheldon and Reichian character types).

The concept of information, on which a systemic phenomenological typology must be based, of course had to be expanded significantly to include an exchange of information that goes beyond what we find in the process of socialization. It had to involve a specifically-structured exchange of information between the generations (it would need to include the ancestors, i.e., the deceased).

As I transitioned from body therapy to phenomenological Systemic Constellation Work, I increasingly saw the Hellinger work as the most advanced, as therapy of a higher order, if the word "therapy" is even appropriate. This work may need to be seen as dealing with the good order in the soul of the individual and in the joint soul of a tribe or family, which goes beyond therapy.[8]

This means that the decisive messages from parents to a child come not only from patterns of behavior and thinking that they have learned themselves, but they form, they shove or dislocate each other in a net of invisible bonds and entanglements, encountering the soul of a child—which is bound by the same net—although at a different place. To work systemically with this means to process this net of entanglements and not only the individual messages. Yet, the messages may refer to the position of the individual in the web of the system.

In my view, we here have a workable bridge for allocating systemic phenomena to the character types.

The type-dependent attitudes, emotions and patterns of behavior can simply be seen phenomenologically as scripts; i.e., stories regarding their systemic informational content. Once Systemic Dynamics have come to light with the help of constellations, the comparison of the frequency of entanglements to the typical patterns can provide indications about the systemic information value of a character type.

Systemic Dynamics Ordered by Character Type

I have carried out this experiment of allocation as best I could, based on my experiences, and came to the following results.

Schizoid structure

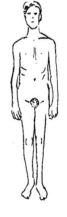

Core convictions in the individual psychological body-character model according to Ron Kurtz[9]: Something is wrong with me. If I show my life force, I am annihilated. / I live on the wrong planet. / I cannot trust my body. / I don't belong here. / I am not welcome here.

Frequently observed parts of systemic dynamics: Interrupted movements toward the mother in very early phases of life (perinatal trauma). Identification with a dead child (sibling, aunt, uncle), especially in cases of murder or late abortions or other events that have been excluded from the family memory. The mother's or grandmother's entanglements with their own mother sur-

rounding miscarriages and stillbirths give rise to a split loyalty between the system of origin (sacrifice of a child) and
the loyalty to one's own present system (which demands
love and life of one's own child), the mother's split loyalty
mirrors the child's situation between existence and nonexistence.

Systemic questions to the system that has become flesh:
i.e., Who was not allowed to exist? Who was not welcome?
Who was annihilated? Who is isolated and who should be
more isolated? Who in the system cannot be trusted? To
whom does the hatred belong? Has someone committed
suicide?

Oral structure

Core convictions:[9] Nobody is there for me. /
Everyone will desert me / I am totally alone. / I
cannot get any support. / I feel as if I have been
weighed and have been found to be too light. /
I can never get enough. **Compensated oral:** I
do not need anyone. / I can do it on my own. /
I do not need any support.

Frequently observed parts of systemic
dynamics: Identification with an excluded child
(early child death, stillbirth, late miscarriage,
etc.), disruptions in the mother's relation to her
own mother=difficulties being a mother (for
example early death of one's own mother).

Systemic questions to the system that has become flesh:
Who (what child) was abandoned, excluded, aborted?
What keeps the mother from being a nurturing mother,
what about the mother's mother? Who has lost a child?
Did any woman die as she gave birth?

Psychopathic structure

Core convictions:[9] Don't force anything onto me. / Do not come too close to me. / You cannot hurt me. / I will show them. / You can be close to me as long as you look up to me. / I never have to show anyone how hurt I am.

Frequently observed parts of systemic dynamics: Disturbed relationship between the parents, both usually entangled in their family of origin and/or in previous partnerships / intimate relationships. Father or mother were not allowed to have a father (alcoholism/addictive structures), the son becomes the mother's hero, etc.

Systemic questions to the system that has become flesh: Is the father present and is he honored? Who in the system has been used and betrayed? Whose anger is circulating in the system? Who in the system was refused respect and recognition?

Masochistic structure

Core convictions:[9] "I am a bad person. / I do everything wrong. / It is hopeless. / Just look at how badly I am doing - please love me. / I have to obey others in order to be loved. / It is not okay to have fun."

Frequently observed parts of systemic dynamics: Guilt dynamics, such as an unjust inheritance of a farm, falsely attributed children, women not honoring the men (father, grandfather), parentification, and generally the family's bearer of burdens.

Systemic questions to the system that has become flesh: Who was dishonored and whose love was hurt? Whose is the hidden anger and who would have had a cause for revenge? Who carries guilt and who should? Who is doing penance for what and who should be? Who was the true victim? Who should have acted and did not act? What was not taken care of in the past? Why are the men in the system seen as the bad guys?

Phallic structure (rigid type 1)

Core convictions:[9] I must work in order to be okay. / There is always something more to do. / I have to watch it, otherwise I will be hurt or used. / I cannot relax or give way. / I have to perform.

Frequently observed parts of systemic dynamics: Disturbed relationship to the father, the father is entangled in his system of origin; held back grief in the system; often this deals with an excluded, hidden, dead person; identification with a dead person.

Systemic questions to the system that has become flesh: In what way did the father not have a father? Who was not good enough for the family? Who is dead and excluded? Whose pain is frozen? What event put what part of the family in a state of shock? Who is missing?

98

Hysterical structure (rigid type 2)

Core convictions:[9] Nobody understands me or listens to me. / My feelings are not acceptable. / I will not follow the feelings of my heart; then you cannot hurt me. / I cannot get the attention that I need.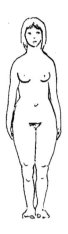

Frequently observed parts of systemic dynamics: Incest and abuse in the system; the child identifies with an earlier partner of the parents or grandparents.

Systemic questions to the system that has become flesh: What wants to be seen? Whose drama must come to light? Who was not seen? Who was betrayed and hurt? What earlier relationship has not been dissolved in peace? With what adult is the child identified?

When I suggest here that we work with the Reichian type model, I do so from the experience of having a remarkably effective orientation tool based on material that has been developed through observation and that was successfully systemically expanded. In my opinion, however, the best possible use of this model in the process of Constellation Work occurs if we are able to forget it entirely or if we let it slip totally into the background during the moment of action. The goal is to provide a space for a holistic perception as we usually do with the orders of love while putting up constellations. The knowledge of the orders of love operates on the background of the overall perception. In the long term, the perceptions modify, expand and supplement the understanding of the orders of love.

This essay was first printed in German in:
The New Magazine for Constellation Work :
Heinz Stark, *"Das leib-haftige Familiensystem"* in

Systemische AufstellungsPraxis, 1, 2005.
Embodied Family Systems
References and Notes

1.Baxa, Essen, Kreszmeyer, (Editor): *Verkörperungen* ["Embodiments"], Heidelberg, 2002
2. Ibid, p. 84 pp
3. You will find some reflections under the keyword "Einzelarbeit" [Individual work] on the website <http://www.starkinstitute.com
4. Wilhelm Reich, *Charakter Analyse* [Character Analysis], Köln 19715
5. Ron Kurtz, *Körperzentrierte Psychotherapie* [Body-oriented Psychotherapy], Essen 1985
6. "In Hakomi Therapy we try to find the information that forms our behavior." (Ibid, p. 247)
7. However, the corresponding experience in the Constellation Work contains many indications that the influences on the character of the child in a systemic context begin already in the mother's womb.
8. In this regard, see the essay: Heinz Stark, *Classical Constellation Work and Movements of the Soul or "Movements of Spirit;" how do they fit together?* In Practice of Systemic Constellations, 2005
9. Ibid, p. 299

6
Family Constellations with Cancer Patients

A young woman in her early thirties, from Europe, is married and living under good circumstances in the United States. She is estranged from her mother, somehow feels inexplicably threatened by her and keeps her at a distance. She is not happy in her marriage, and does not know if she should stay or leave. She is not considering having children; instead she is concerned about her interrupted career. She is moved by the idea of having a child, but this issue is accompanied by a certain fear.

This was her situation when she came to an introductory workshop of my two-year training course for Systemic Family Constellations in California. She decided to participate in the entire training course. After a short time as a trainee, a cancer growth was discovered on her cervix.

Since working with the essential life problems of all participants is an integral part of the training concept, during the course of the two years we worked with different areas of her current system and especially with her family of origin.

The intense and deep Family Constellation Work proved to be very effective here. The client now feels very much at home in her marriage, she feels close to her mother, and she is the happy mother of a healthy boy. The cancerous growth has disappeared.

Does this mean Family Constellation Work can heal cancer?

Nobody really knows what causes the many miracles of healing. It is a fact that sometimes, against all the expectations of doctors, spontaneous healing of cancer does occur, even in advanced stages of the illness. One of many possible questions here would be, "What strengthened her body's defense mechanisms so suddenly, or why had they been so greatly weakened before?"

It is also a fact that solving subconscious entanglements in a family system often has an amazing effect and solves all kinds of life problems, turning them to the better. Illnesses are a very sustained form of manifesting life problems.

One thing is obvious: in order to achieve deep solutions it is usually not enough to see a human being as simply a *physical* being.

I found the most encompassing perspective for looking at unfavorable events in the life of a person within Systemic Family Constellations, as developed by Bert Hellinger. This approach goes beyond psychosomatics and even beyond psychotherapies that see the self as holistic (for example Postural Integration, my old home base within body-oriented psychotherapy). Even modern schools of family therapy that take consideration of the interactions within social systems are again expanded considerably.

In Family Constellation Work we are watching interactive events in which balancing processes are experienced that involve several generations and time levels. This includes not only the effects that those who are alive have on each other, but also the effects that originate in those who are dead, in their destinies and their disastrous actions during their lifetimes. This continues to have an effect on the family system, usually without the persons involved know-

102

ing about it, and without the entangled persons ever having known each other previously.

In the example mentioned earlier in this essay, which involved a cancer patient, it turned out that a child died after birth through the culpability of its mother (the client's great-grandmother on her mother's side) and this incident and, the existence of that child, were erased from the conscious family memory, but the unknowingly working conscious of the system never forgets, it secretly passed on all the way down the generations to the subconscious of the client.

The client was deeply connected to the dead child, so deeply that she subliminally experienced what the child experienced, namely having its life threatened, being afraid of its own mother, not being allowed to live its life freely, being unseen, unloved and separated from the community of the family (especially from siblings and parents).

At the same time she had a deep, loving connection to her great-grandmother, to whom she ultimately owes her life. She was connected to her great-grandmother's guilt and to her striving for atonement, to her shame and her misfortune. She was stuck in atonement behavior for the actions of her great-grandmother and thereby relinquished family happiness of her own and success in her career.

The suffering aspects in the life of the client, which at first seemed to be separate and independent of each other, suddenly all made sense and showed themselves in their context.

I have found, in addition to other information, the form in which an illness expresses itself (here a carcinoma) often provides access to the systemic events. It makes sense to see the mental, energetic or spiritual web of connections that we find between those belonging to a family or a tribe as one joint organism.

If I, as the practitioner, open up to the appearance of the symptom in the bodily organism of the client and let it impact me, and then project it into the larger organism of the system, then this often gives me the direction from which I can approach the Constellation Work.

Cancer is life in the form of enormous cell divisions and growth processes that in the tumor are initially fully insulated from the rest of the organism. It grows in the middle of the organism, but it is isolated from it, excluded, and yet it threatens the whole. This raises the question: What piece of life is this that is so dangerous for the entire organism that it has to be excluded, and yet it remains a part of the whole?

In our case, we saw a growth on the cervix, raising the issues of birth and death. The validity of this way of thinking is illustrated by the following example:

During a routine checkup, a seventy-five year old therapist in my training group in Wisconsin was surprised to learn that she had a cancer growth in her connective tissue—the term "connective" is very interesting in this context.

This led to the question of what split-off, excluded life she may have been connected with? The answer came quickly in a moving and dramatic constellation. Exactly at the place on her hip where the growth was, she experienced a deep contact to a twin sister, with whom she is intimately connected, although she never before in her life had received any conscious information about this.

Incidentally, before the constellation she had agreed to undergo chemotherapy, which was carried out in several treatment phases after the constellation. The tumor disappeared very quickly and one almost had the impression that the chemotherapy walked through open doors. According to the impressions of all those involved, she also survived the side effects of the medicine surprisingly well, considering her advanced age.

To mention yet a third basic experience with cancer within Constellation Work, I would like to return to the client in California whom I mentioned in the beginning. As has been shown, the type of symptom and its place of appearance could serve to clarify the systemic entanglement. In addition, the essence of the illness also contains the energy of the systemic dynamics. The illness is, so to speak, charged with forces that stem from the larger organism and that find their expression in different ways. We see a life-destroying energy at work that is often connected with guilt from acts that have been committed, but a guilt that has not been accepted. This is a self-destructive process that functions as a kind of substitute atonement. At the same time it wanders around lost in the system and is evidently seeking to be taken over, all the way down to the grand-children.

"Can Illness Be Love?" is therefore the title of one of my series of seminars that has grown out of exactly these types of experiences. "Yes, I will take that on," is the decision made deep in the soul of the child who is born later on and who, in its deep love and connection, is prepared to take on any sacrifice necessary.

How far this can go is illustrated by the following story about a woman from Northern Germany (she was also in her mid-thirties).

She came for an individual session to my practice afflicted with thyroid cancer. We found and solved a dynamic on the paternal side of the system. I also had the opportunity to work directly with the father regarding this dynamic during a constellation seminar. The cancer disappeared without a trace relatively quickly. Over a year later the woman returned, this time with breast cancer. According to the doctors, this was a kind of cancer that did not have anything to do with the thyroid cancer that had disappeared, i.e., it represented a new cancer illness.

Again we found a serious entanglement involving the client, this time on the maternal side of the family.

(Unfortunately, I have not yet had any feedback on what happened next, and I sincerely hope that after our work she is able to express her deep love and connection to her loved ones in a conscious and life-affirming way.)

In conclusion I would like to describe another very recent constellation experience, in which all elements that were outlined above came together. A fifty-three-year-old woman from Southern Germany, a mother of three children, suffered from breast cancer.

When she appeared in my constellation seminar, one breast had already been removed. When she spoke of this, she broke out in tears, but at the same time I intuited a sense of satisfaction in her expression. When I mentioned this to her, she became aware of it and confirmed that she had a deep feeling of "now I've paid, I've sacrificed my breast and that is enough now." In addition to this clear indication of a guilt and atonement dynamic, she told me two tumors were found in her breast, and they were very different in character (in their form and in the structure of the tissue). One of them is soft and rather diffuse, whereas the other one was hard and had sharp contours.

In order to begin the constellation, I suggested that she choose a representative for herself, and one for each tumor. For one tumor she chose a man and for the other one she chose a woman. As is the case so often in constellation images that depict the relationship between the symptom and the person who has the symptom, the representative for the client turned away and did not want to watch.

Which events in the system had not been looked at became clear within thirty minutes, independently of each other, based on two independent focal points.

The "male tumor" stared at a point on the floor and his perceptions indicated war and violence. Events led us to a point where it became obvious that we were in the middle of the father's dramatic war experience as a "partisan hunter" in Italy. What the representative for the tumor was looking at turned out to be what the father had to look at: a victim, a woman who writhed in pain on the floor, expressed through a female representative.

"I felt like this victim, partly dismembered, and would have wanted to place a knife in the father's hand so that he could put an end to my (and our) life suffering," said the representative. The father was in despair between his guilt as a perpetrator and at the same time he was full of empathy and could obviously not allow himself to commit a mercy killing. The daughter, the client, felt deeply connected to both the victim and the father. She was a loving daughter and was prepared to atone for his guilt by dying in agony with the victim.

On the other side of the constellation events, the "female tumor" introduced an abuse and incest dynamic, which unfolded in the maternal line of the family of origin. Here, an entanglement had arisen that was similar to the one described in the first example, the young woman who lived in California.

When I look back on my many years of experience with Constellation Work and focus on the cancer cases that were dealt with, I believe I can rightfully say that Systemic Family Constellations are an exceptionally valuable aid when it comes to promoting healing processes in people who are ill with cancer.

The publication in Germany of this essay is in
preparation and will be released in spring 2006
(see www.starkinstitute.com)

7
Two Strategies—One Modality:
Classical Constellation Work and Movements of the
Soul or "Movements of Spirit,"
How Do They Fit Together?

Diverging Tendencies in the Constellation Movement

Not long ago, in grey prehistory, when we lived in "the land of the wind that lifted many kites,"[1] and when we were united and led philosophically by Bert Hellinger himself, we strived to avoid creating a church for the newly-started movement of systemic constellations and everything that inevitably goes with such a church, such as believers of the right faith and heretics, cultists, and those who are leaving the church, of course. But now it seems to me as if something like this is actually happening.

I am here deliberately referring to the metaphor of the church, which came from Bert himself, and I must come back to it later, when I touch upon the concept of the "Movement of Spirit" which was introduced by Bert.

The first time that I began to be aware of the diverging tendencies in the international constellation movement, was during the international conference "Conflict Fields, Knowing Fields" in 2001 in Würzburg, Germany.

As I had been asked to do, I offered an introductory workshop in English about working with movable elements or, as I call them, indicating elements in order to show what the results are in classical Constellation Work.

Here I believe it is necessary to briefly describe what the terms used are supposed to mean.

The term "classical Constellation Work" is used for the process of constellations as we learned it from Bert Hellinger during the early 1990s in which the constellation facilitators move the representatives in a seeking and rearranging way, in order to find a solving image and process for the client.

This occurs when the facilitator opens up to the events in phenomenological openness, sounding out what appears depending on the extent of their knowledge about the orders of life and their own empirical experiences. They thereby carefully follow the information that is made available through the emerging systemic memory field.

The movable elements of which I spoke are regular representatives and can move around freely in the constellation without being asked to do so, and they are often abstract elements, such as guilt, the symptom, etc.

The free elements should not be confused with what we have learned to call movements of the soul—these are slow, trancelike movements by the representatives or by the person seeking a solution, which can bring something to light from the depths of the system—something that can be expected to contribute to a solution.

However, experience shows that the transitions between movable elements and movements of the soul are very fluid, which is not unimportant for our further considerations.

I thus understood my task of leading an introductory workshop as being to carry out classical Constellation Work and to thereby introduce one of the many variations that, at the time, had recently been developed.

I might add that even after many years of intense international training activity, I still cannot imagine a meaningful alternative to the classical type of constellation as a didactic concept for introducing the meaning and conveying an understanding of phenomenological Systemic Constellation Work.

The seminar in Würzburg went very well in all aspects, the function of the movable elements as an aid was made very clear, and we were able to find a very good solution for the client.

Once the applause had died down and we started with questions and answers, an angry American woman stood up and asked me with a trembling voice, how I dare to move the people back and forth. She was in no way satisfied by my explanations and, almost as a way of making me shut up she, said: "Bert never moves representatives back and forth; he always lets the people move themselves!" This was a mental uppercut, which actually made me stagger a bit. . . .

It suddenly became clear to me that a new generation of international constellation facilitators was emerging under the direct guidance of Bert Hellinger, for whom "Movements of the Soul" or the "Movements of Spirit" as Bert calls his process now, is the only modality of Constellation Work.

This still makes me dismayed, sad and concerned, and I have never really understood the reason for the devaluation of our successful work, which lasted for many years.

When Bert officially introduced the new procedure once in Linz,[2] at the time I was happy about the exciting extension of the Constellation Work, which was to be explored, but I was not happy about the replacement of Systemic Constellations with a new, different type of Constellation Work.

Against the Devaluation of Classical Family Constellations

In Garmisch-Partenkirchen Bert Hellinger held a lecture entitled: "Go with Spirit—Family Constellations as Applied Life Philosophy."[3]

Bert's modesty could be seen when he placed himself into the row of constellation facilitators and said that he now believes that he is just one among many who are doing this.

However, this attitude does not say anything about the impact and the influence Bert's thoughts and actions have on the whole movement of constellation facilitators.

In many hearts and minds he is simply *the* authority in the area of phenomenological constellations. This can be seen perhaps most clearly wherever there are attempts at distancing oneself and turning away from Bert. (Today you can find program flyers in Germany from well-known facilitators that don't mention the name of Bert Hellinger anymore).

In the article mentioned, Bert speaks about classical constellations and says that it has brought many blessings. But in the context of the entire lecture, it sounds something like this: *well, at the time, when we didn't know better, this type of work brought many blessings.*

In my work, however, and I know in the work of many good facilitators, this procedure *still brings many blessings today.*

Based on my experiences, treating family constellations as a commendable but prehistoric model of therapy, and as a type of psychotherapy that is outdated, cannot remain unchallenged in this form.

Of course my family constellations and those of other experienced constellation facilitators have developed further and today, in many aspects, look different than they did in 1993, and yet there are essential elements that have remained constant. If I were to rely exclusively on the method of "Movements of the Soul," this would represent a great loss of excellent healing tools.

If I, for example, take the case of a young woman who took part in my constellation training in California for two years, it becomes clear to me how important a good accord between all constellation varieties is to a comprehensive success.

She did not really know what to do with her life; she was weak and did not have a good relationship with her husband, she was estranged from her parents in Europe, and she was afraid at the thought of ever having a child. She also had a malignant abscess on her cervix.

During the two years I worked with her on different layers and dynamics in her family with movements of the soul, with classical Constellation Work and various creative ways of constellation modalities, I also set up constellations three times with her mother and twice with her husband.

The young woman now has a very beautiful relationship with her husband, she is the happiest and proudest mother of a healthy child that one can imagine, and the cancer growth is gone.

"Movements of the Soul" and classical Constellation Work here proved to be equally effective and they supplemented each other mutually as good tools in supporting her healing.

If, for example, a client presents a totally unclear set of symptoms, which leaves the facilitator with more questions than impulses about which direction to take, the movement of the soul can often lead to an enlightening unfolding of very unexpected dynamics. But there are areas in which the methods that have been developed from classical Constellation Work are unbeatable.

As an example, finding miscarriages or abortions from earlier or extramarital relationships is eminently important, of course, especially to dissolve any representation that leads to a reduction in life quality. In this sense, the precise arrangement of siblings, uncles and aunts, even sometimes great-uncles and great-aunts, into the order of the system is important for achieving psychological stability, and is important for the work of letting go of the childish desire to take the burden off one's mother or father.

As an example, it was necessary to create a doubling of a beloved grandmother who became a child murderess, into the life-giving part of the ancestor, who is and will continue to be loved, honored and respected and, on the other hand, the perpetrator part. This part had to be accepted, even approved of in terms of this special aspect of the fate of the grandmother. It was then necessary to give back the guilt and atonement to the grandmother whereby, at the same time, the love of the client towards the grandmother could reach a new level.

An important step was to de-identify the client from the victim. Other important steps were to bring the father of the killed child into the family system, to support the client's stabilizing, to finally create a felt sense of belonging in the row of siblings, and for the client to accept the father. Ultimately, it became possible for her to finally move toward the mother.

The reason I am describing these necessary steps of the soul in such detail—methods that of themselves are well known—is in order that we remember the range of layers that need to be addressed.

Based on my experience, I doubt that constellations that consist exclusively of "Movements of the Soul" will ever have the necessary complexity that could provide all necessary initial impulses for an encompassing healing process of a complex web of entanglements.

Therapy and Healing vs. Life Abundance?

When Bert says the current form of his work is not about solving problems or healing, but ultimately about life in its abundance,[4] I ask myself however, from my healing perspective that is focused on one's entire life, if constellations were not always about life in its abundance? Did I understand anything wrong during my first learning years, when I followed Bert around the world because there were no trainings?

Has the starting point of the work not always been a desire for solution and healing? At least when people come to me for family constellations, there is always something that is not okay, something that is no longer whole, and something that will make life whole needs to happen. Nobody comes just for the fun of it.

Anyone who comes to a one-on-one session or to a constellation seminar has an issue or a request. Taking their requests seriously means taking the people seriously. Their requests describe my mandate.

When someone pays me for working on his/her issue in a seminar or in a one-on-one session, I enter into a contractual agreement, an agreement of exchange, wherein my service consists of working to the best of my ability to deal with the issue.

However, "to the best of my ability" means to use all my knowledge and all the healing tools and methods that I have, i.e., to ultimately place myself in the service of the greater striving for solution, which is indicated by the individual issue.

This is true independent of the process, which then may be used in this marriage of convenience. Certainly we do not usually meet in an exclusive club to explore "applied life philosophy." So whatever happens, in a therapeutic setting a special space in which there are clients and issues is created for initiating healing processes.

If, within the framework of his/her therapy with a client, a therapist might have the idea to pray, then within this context this would be considered to be therapy, even if it may go beyond the framework of what usually occurs during therapy.

If Bert now tells us that by using the movements of the soul we enter depths that go far beyond psychotherapy, then I of course have no problems agreeing with that, to the extent we are dealing with mindsets, attitudes and behavior—but not in relationship to what we do, for there nothing in our frame of reference has changed.

When it comes to going beyond narrow methodological psychotherapeutic boundaries I cannot differentiate between movements of the soul and classically-oriented Constellation Work. It too goes far beyond traditional methods when it comes to its approach, its phenomenological focus and its multi-generational perspective.

In my basic attitude, which was formed through classical constellations, I remain focused on my clients' issues and their desire for healing.

In my experience, issues are the entrances to healing spaces. There are different entrances to various healing spaces at different levels, and yet they are all a part of one and the same large building. I let the client lead me to this entrance and I encourage him/her to open it as soon as we have found a key that fits.

In these spaces we enter into with our clients in order to meet the ones that they are connected with, whether alive or dead long ago, the facilitators are more like servants than lords. We serve by following the progress of the solution process and simply the good progress of life itself. If this should reveal an even greater design, we humbly bow our heads.

A Different, Larger Force Takes over the Guidance of the Constellation Process

Let us continue to follow Bert Hellinger's arguments in his lecture entitled "Going with Spirit," regarding the characteristics of the movement process:

> Here, a different power has taken command. I give myself to this force and suddenly I know whether I must do something and what I must do, even if at first it seems absurd. But I go along with this movement, and then something happens that one could not have anticipated.[5]

I think this quote takes us to a junction in our discussion.

Everything Bert says here largely agrees with my own experience. Here, a different power has taken command. It has taken command—not taken over my power of judgment and not my responsibility for fulfilling my contract with my client. It is a different power, i.e., different than my own will but, in the context of the lecture, the meaning of Bert's words is that *obviously a different power is active in the movement of the soul than is active in classical constellations.*

Is this really so?

Have we not learned to put ourselves into a state which Bert so beautifully calls the "empty center?" In this state we have arrived at a determinant point in the process of finding solutions, in which we experience full stupidity and helplessness and are at the mercy of the unleashed or resisting powers of the system. We stand there knowing nothing, willing to give up any type of structuring, when suddenly something unexpected happens, maybe something totally unbelievable, something that goes further, maybe even something dangerous that leads us onward. We then follow this guidance carefully, still doubting, always testing, but we follow it. . . .

In my view, those who do not know this state and who do not seek this state during the constellation process have not understood the essence of Constellation Work.

The major sin in classical Constellation Work against the profound depths which according to Bert are brought to light through the movements of the soul, is to intervene—at least to intervene too early—in a process of movement that unfolds all by itself. In Bert's view, this unfolding is guided by a higher power, which means that any intervention gives the impression of being nothing short of hubris.

I ask myself, however, why this wonderful force that I see in both types of Constellation Work can only guide the representatives and not the facilitators? And why it only expresses itself in movements and not, for example, in the form of my intuition.

I can only state that this power, a power that I privately call the self-healing power of the system, is so strong that it goes beyond the limitations of my mind, implants thoughts that were previously not there, or for example makes me forget representations ("How, what . . . who was here . . . father . . . grandfather?") I have by now learned to read this confusion as information, as a possible sign of a generational confusion.

This force puts my body in strange states, and I may, for example, feel extremely nauseous ("Oh, I sense that I may have stumbled upon an incestuous system.")

In general I am astonished at my own strange way of behaving, which is totally unthinkable in my everyday life. I find myself in a mood of almost limitless patience, which is foreign to me, and I have a deep trust that everything will unfold and make a turn for the good.

This force helps me to move through the constellation, often for a long time in an almost trance-like state, and to have the courage to follow what appears, even if it appears to be unbelievable. In this state all my senses are fully open and, at the same time, the mind is operating at full speed.

Suddenly I know that I have to wait—simply wait—or else to do something very specific, and then I wonder why I am bringing in this new representative right now. It is only later that I see how important it was. Or else I make a mistake that normally is just stupid, and yet it gives the whole process a turn that provides a solution. Or suddenly a participant in the outer circle falls from his chair and lands inside the circle and thus fills the place of a missing representative, or else a participant begins to quiver and cry on her chair.

I perceive both a strong systemic memory field as well as a power that guides me and carries me, using me in the service of its striving toward solution. These are different powers and yet they are the same; they transform into each other.

My knowledge, my intuition and my willingness to be guided all merge with this power. So does the information from the representatives—the memory of what has been said previously or a gesture, a strange statement that suddenly makes sense, a body posture, a movement of the hand, a glance, a strong feeling and, as soft music in the background, we also have the issue that has initiated our actions.

As is the case with the movements of the soul, it takes time and patience for these forces to unfold fully. The slogan from the late 1990s, that *a constellation is good if it has few representatives and if it is short*, has here totally lost its validity.

If we apply Bert Hellinger's language on what has been described above, this kind of a family constellation cannot be described as a movement *of* the soul, but as a movement *in* the soul. It is a movement in one's own soul, out of one's own soul, through the healing and guiding powers of the larger soul of the family (the system), which has here opened up and in which we are moving.

But this simply means that, in essence, family constellations and movements of the soul are one and the same.

Regarding Problems and Limitations of Both Methods

The dangers inherent in classically-oriented constellations are, of course, clear to see and Bert is right to refer to them in his lecture,[6] probably from his own experience. For if we are guided simply by our own ideas, we will not get far or deep. If we are not able to provide enough space for the forces that are active in the system to take effect, we either land in a dead end street and have to break off the constellation, or we come to a solution that is not convincing and that comes more from a cognitive explanatory context after the fact, than from any impulse toward an effective solution on the part of the client.

In my trainings, it is therefore very important to promote the abilities to allow oneself to be guided and carried in such a process.

This may sound complicated and, of course, one may ask if it's worth all the trouble, if in essence we only have to sit there patiently and let the larger power take over the field in the hope that it will take care of everything.

This raises another question: Is it really clear that the movements of the soul always follow a suitable course and do they always lead to healing results? Of course, one may take the attitude that, in view of the fact that one is being guided by a greater power, these pragmatic questions are irrelevant.

However, since we do not know what this power is, and since we must at least allow for the possibility that the effect of this power is not totally independent of contextual factors, we need at least some criteria to determine if the process is taking a comprehensible course.

In our situation, the immediate context is our client's system. In principle it is possible that the forces in the system, for whatever reasons, do not desire that the issue be dealt with or a solution be found and that they lead us astray. In other words, the systemic resistance gains the upper hand and wins out over the striving for a solution.

Here is an example: in a training group with very experienced representatives, a movement of the soul begins to unfold in a trance-like way. One of the main persons was the client's grandmother and her movements clearly gave the impression that she was seeking something, and she did this consistently. After a while it seemed meaningful to put up a representative for whatever was sought.

The two of them then began to relate to each other, and there followed a never-ending movement of coming together and of separation, like a couple that cannot come together but that cannot leave each other either. Since I really wanted to find out if this movement would naturally lead to the next level, I left it alone for a long time. Their game grew more intense.

Slowly, but surely, I had to doubt these movements would ever lead us to something deeper. The client, on the other hand, had very intense issues and, in comparison, what appeared in the constellation (movement of the soul) seemed to be very superficial. This simple perception alone could seem to constitute controlling the process.

The preliminary interview and other signs had led me to assume that the problem originated in the mother of the mother, and that is how she was chosen to be the main protagonist. Without knowledge about orders and systemic phenomenological experience, I would first of all not be able to make a correct selection of the members of the system that are to be represented, and I would also have felt helplessly at the mercy of what simply appeared.

Now, afterwards, I am glad that I trusted my experiences with classical Constellation Work and not this *movement of distraction*. I followed my suspicion and placed a representative of a dead child in front of her feet. What then followed was truly deep and clarifying.

It turned out the client was burdened by a serious multiple identification: she carried the murderess in her—the victim and the guilt—as well as the perpetrator's striving for atonement.

This client is doing very well today.

The constellations that were necessary in order to arrive at a comprehensive solution were so varied, as I already mentioned, I doubt that a pure movement of the soul would have met such complexity.

During my personal attempts at finding solution, a movement of the soul was carried out under the auspices of a very experienced colleague, using excellent representatives. It was wonderful, the movements brought details to light for me, and I understood the source of a certain behavior, which is valuable and important to me. There was only one thing that this deep movement did not give me, and that was a solution to my urgent issue.

After one and a half years of waiting patiently, I decided to visit a traditionally-oriented constellation facilitator in this matter. This experience left me liberated and, on top of it all, with overflowing love in my heart, whereas up to then it had been kept in a state of dull endurance and suffering. This constellation took only fifteen minutes. Of course the second session was a further supplement to the first, but it was the determinant step, and it did not come from the movement during the first session itself.

Afterwards I asked myself why my colleague, who was so experienced, did not do what was necessary? I suspect that I know why. He was kept from doing so by an unseen law that lingers in many heads, but that was, to my knowledge, never formulated by Bert: *Do not intervene!*

But I ask myself, what would speak against sometimes taking supporting measures at the end of a constellation which are based on the movement of the soul? In my case it was a deeply-felt giving back of guilt that I was carrying, for wrong reasons, to the person whose guilt it was.

Here, there is something more to consider. In my case, the movement of the soul did not contain any indications about my specific entanglement; it showed a systemic scene of a dramatic event that did not really have anything to do with my own entanglement.

The colleague could only have come up with a supplemental intervention from experiences with classical Constellation Work, i.e., from what in such cases is often required or simply from the continuation of the work with the methods of classically-oriented constellations.

So what could have been wrong with that? Maybe economic or time-economic conditions, or maybe a kind of belief in miracles, in the healing power of the magical beautiful movement of the soul? Are we not here confusing depth with effect?

In my case, we did see life in its abundance, but since I would prefer to live life in its abundance rather than only watch it, I am dependent on finding solutions. If we want sustainable solutions, it is necessary to deal as best we can with the entire complexity of illness-creating or, seen from a different perspective, healing factors.

In addition, the events that occur must in some way be meaningfully related to my problem, and the process must truly be relevant within the systemic structure of the strained web of relationships.

This means that the work with movements in Constellation Work will not succeed without a certain amount of process control and feedback to the framework. Frameworks are created for instance by the issue, or by the symptoms in the person seeking solution, as well as by the frame of reference of previous experiences.

If something becomes visible during the process of movements that exceeds what could have been expected, then that which exceeds is measured by what one maybe could have expected, and only in this way can it be recognized as something that goes beyond what was expected.

The Interaction

The reception and communication of the events during a constellation has great methodological importance for the effect on the person seeking solution. As a rule, the burdened client is, of course, not subjected to the process from a neutral state, holding his empty center. The client is under tension and during the entire process, constant attempts to interpret and categorize will occur in his/her head: "What does that mean? Who is doing that?" etc.

If no mediation occurs by identifying and commenting on crucial points during the process, clients can virtually get lost in the events and despair. I am not referring to rash, restricting interpretations by the facilitator. On the contrary, keeping interpretations open, enduring this state and surrendering to the process, can also be an important part of the verbal contact between the facilitator and the client, so that the constellation process can become a joint learning process of body, mind and spirit.

Movements reach limits where they come to a temporary or permanent standstill. Here it can be meaningful to question the representatives, to introduce a new person, or to relax a situation that has gotten stuck by regrouping. After some time of joint contemplation, a new movement suddenly emerges from the current constellation, which ultimately can lead to movements of the soul and classic constellations flowing organically into each other, as was indicated above with the free elements. The opportunities that come from the movement, and the necessity of addressing the problem layers in a differentiated and encompassing way, can thus interact beautifully and very economically.

This is especially successful if we build up the constellation successively. Maybe the representative of the client begins to move first, then the parents do so too, (which usually shows the side of the family in which the entanglements can be found) and then maybe some other important persons. It is quite possible that as the number of representatives increases the constellation continues to move around certain focal points, while other more order-related representatives standing still, right from the beginning or after their movements have calmed down. All of a sudden we can see the movements of the soul within a classical constellation.

What happens now with the stance of fossilized classical constellation vs progressive movement of the soul?

The "Movements of Spirit"
I would like to counteract the tendency toward mystification of the movement process.

For a long time now, various body-oriented therapies have used the concept of "body flow" to describe trance-like movements, which are experienced as being moved through an involuntary force, which then takes over a kind of guiding function. There, the understanding is that the wisdom of the body has taken charge and, in this way, expresses subconscious contents and corresponding feelings.

In Java there is a dancing tradition that includes involuntary movements, placing them within an open spiritual context (Prabto). Some years ago I ran into the same phenomenon in connection with Qi Gong. In the Biyun Qi Gong School there is an Elements Qi Gong, in which one aligns oneself with the directions and colors based on the five Chinese elements. After some initiating Qi Gong movements, one finds oneself moved by the Qi life force, which leads to all kinds of surprising experiences. West African tribes have these trance-like movement events, which are similar to our constellations, which they use to solve acute problems in the village community—for example, in order to find a perpetrator.

All these examples make it easy to recognize that what happens and how it is interpreted is highly dependent on the context within which it occurs. Our special context consists of human systems and the use of representatives, which we have learned from experiences with classical family constellations.

In Bert's latest development he calls the work with moving representatives "Movements of Spirit." However, the power that is operating is no longer seen in terms of its context, but it is placed before the context, and it becomes something *a priori*—something divine—an elemental force from which everything emerges and proceeds.

With his increasing experience of practical Constellation Work, he sees this change as being necessary. Bert thus, in principle, abandons the systemic idea, which in essence begins with interactions, and he also abandons the phenomenological approach, which stays away from any predetermined theories or other *a priori* statements.

He has thereby abandoned a platform on which we all could move around. I was therefore quite curious about the practical experiences that had caused such a far-reaching development, i.e., examples that Bert bases it on. When I then read his lecture, I was astonished.

As an example, he cites the victims of rape, or victims of abuse and says: "If I go with Spirit, then I see the so-called perpetrators at the same level as the so-called victims. I see them as people of the same kind. They have different origins and different entanglements, but they have the same right."

This I understood precisely. I sensed it deeply and I have for many years now been using this without knowing anything about the movements of Spirit, for they were not even discovered or invented back then. So from whom did I learn it? I learned it from Bert Hellinger during the time of classical constellations.

Another example: A client complains about the bad things that he or she experienced during childhood. So I now look at this power philosophically and ask the client to also look at his/her situation philosophically and say: "Whatever happened, thank you. I take it as a power. I take these parents as these special ones, who gave me this special power that is essential to my life." Suddenly everything that had happened is transfigured. It becomes precious.

That is beautiful, it has power, it also gave me power and I have been using this type of reframing in my work ever since the beginning of the nineties. And whom did I learn this from? I learned it from Bert Hellinger during the times of the classical family constellations.

Obviously, the experience with constellations has not changed essentially but the frame of reference, the context in which Bert places his work, has: it is an elemental force, a divine *a priori*. It has a powerful effect not only in constellations, but all the way from the development of the facilitator movement to the overall movement of the world. At the same time, he provides an explanation for why peace is impossible. He says, "and if we look at things the way they are, it becomes very clear that the divine or the elemental power—the power that moves the world—wants conflict."[7]

127

This new frame of reference is based on a philosophical reasoning in which Bert places himself in the tradition of Process-Philosophy, which spans from Heraclites to Alfred North Whitehead to today. But in this philosophical approach there are two basic, essentially opposing directions. One might be called the evolutionary direction and the other the more metaphysical, teleological, even theological direction.

Bert's choice of words leaves no doubt about the philosophical direction he has taken with the "movements of Spirit." Spirit is the driver of the world itself and maybe something like the Holy Ghost; Telos stands for what is Good.

Not long ago I facilitated a workshop in a Catholic convent in Canada. There, I found a flyer in which one of the nuns offered a workshop entitled: *Liturgical Dance: Movement with the Spirit.* The flyer read, "The spirit of God can move our heart, minds and bodies . . . ." Here, being moved is offered as a special form of prayer, devotion and a way of "being with God" and being "moved by God."

As we can see, Bert is no longer so far from his old home.

Of course his beliefs, his convictions, his perceptions are all rightfully and understandably his own; we all often experience something very impressive in the movements of the soul and, in the moment of healing, we feel the presence of the Holy.

But we did this already from the beginning of the Constellation Work. I found it incredibly helpful to learn from Bert that the highest religious attitude was to simply pause in awe and honor of the phenomena themselves, and not to barge on ahead and get involved with what we cannot know, so that we do not belittle it.

It is clear to me that systems theory, with its main categories of the reduction of complexity, represents a very feeble basis for understanding the world. Yet, I did find it well chosen, since the contextual limitations of a model of interaction protected us from ideological fights and from the founding of a church. This danger, however, is now real and present, if the events during constellations are theologized.

So I am pleading not only for the development of a respectful interplay between movements of the soul and the mode of operation that is based on classical constellations, but also for our coming together on the solid, proven platform called phenomenological Systemic Constellation Work based on Bert Hellinger's discoveries.

Even if Bert agrees with Heraclitus, that war is the father of all things, we can also see that humanity's great life-promoting projects, for example the building of dikes along our coasts, came about through cooperation, and that the previous statement, which comes from a patriarchal slave holder society, requires at least a supplement:

If war is the father of all things—then peace is the mother of all life.

This essay was first published in German in
Praxis der Systemaufstellung, 1, 2005, p. 17pp

Two Strategies—One Modality
Resources and Notes

1. *"Derselbe Wind lässt viele Drachen steigen"*, ["The Same Wind Lifts Many Kites"] Title of the 2nd Work Conference of the IAG, 1999; book with the same title (Conference Report) Editor: Gunthard Weber, Carl-Auer-Systeme Verlag, 2001 Heidelberg.
2. At the invitation of Bert Hellinger, a work conference about the "Movement of the Soul" was held in Linz.
3. Systemic Constellation Practice, 2004, Vol. 2, p. 14
4. Ibid, p. 16
5. Ibid, p. 15
6. Ibid, p. 15
7. Ibid, p. 16

About Heinz Stark

Heinz Stark has been instrumental in bringing Systemic Constellation Work to America since 1995. Stark is a systemic body and family therapist in private practice in Germany. He has been incorporating Art, Bio-energetics, Gestalt Therapy, Postural-Integration and Shamanic approaches in his practice.

In the early nineties, Stark began to integrate Bert Hellinger's phenomenological systemic approach in his work. Heinz Stark is now one of the leading teachers of this work in Germany. He is one of the very few teachers offering a training and certification program in the U.S. For that purpose he founded The Orders of Life Association with the intention to provide the highest quality education in Systemic Constellation Work.

For additional information about Heinz Stark, training in Systemic Constellation Work, or the Stark Institute, visit www.starkinstitute.com.